LIVING A SUCCESSFUL LIFE TODAY

(Includes Study Guide)

By
DERRICK R. RHODES

Copyright © 2012 by Derrick R. Rhodes

Living A Successful Life Today
by Derrick R. Rhodes

Printed in the United States of America

ISBN 9781624190285

All rights reserved solely by the author. The author guarantees all contents are original and do not infringe upon the legal rights of any other person or work. No part of this book may be reproduced in any form without the permission of the author. The views expressed in this book are not necessarily those of the publisher.

Unless otherwise indicated, Bible quotations are taken from The New International Version, The Message, The New Revised Standard Version, The New King James Version and the New Living Translation.

www.xulonpress.com

In honor of my granddaughter, Sanaai Rhodes;
my grandmother, Lillian P. Rhodes;
and my mother-in-law, Christine Davis.

CONTENTS

Introduction:	Steps to Living a Successful Life Today, Part 1	vii
Chapter 1	Steps to Living a Successful Life Today, Part 2	29
Chapter 2	Steps to Living a Successful Life Today, Part 3	44
Chapter 3	Reigniting Your Passion for God, Part 1	58
Chapter 4	Reigniting Your Passion for God, Part 2	74
Chapter 5	Managing Stress, Part 1	92
Chapter 6	Managing Stress, Part 2	109
Chapter 7	When You Can't See Your Way Clear, Part 1	126
Chapter 8	When You Can't See Your Way Clear, Part 2	145
Chapter 9	Guidelines for Leading a Study	161

INTRODUCTION

Steps to a Successful Life Today, Part 1

———⊗⊗⊗———

READ SCRIPTURE: Philippians 4:10-13
I rejoice in the Lord greatly that now at last you have revived your concern for me; indeed, you were concerned for me, but had no opportunity to show it. Not that I am referring to being in need; for I have learned to be content with whatever I have. I know what it is to have little, and I know what it is to have plenty. In any and all circumstances I have learned the secret of being well-fed and of going hungry, of having plenty and of being in need. I can do all things through him who strengthens me.

Do you want to live a successful life? Do you want to live a triumphant life? From the opening bell of our lives, trials and tribulations stalk us; they repeatedly back us into a corner, but no one starts out saying to himself "I'm going to lose this fight," "I want to be a failure," "I want my life to be fruitless," "I want my life to be a disaster."

Maybe this statement is too general—that people don't start off their lives saying "I want to be a failure"—but no one I can think of begins by wanting to be unsuccessful.

As I watch television, listen to the news, read the newspaper, and hear people's gripes and grumbles, I realize that although many of us want to live a successful life we are not. Too many of us feel we are living an unsuccessful life, not reaching our goals, not crossing the finish line, not sprouting into what we feel in our hearts we should be.

Successful living has dodged too many of us. Could that be you? Do you feel as if you are unsuited to living a successful life? Do you feel as if you haven't accomplished what God created you to do? Do you believe you could do more, should be doing more, want to do more?

Maybe you don't. It might not be you. But it's someone you know. Someone you know who looks successful, looks as though they have it all together, looks like they have everything a person could ever want—houses, cars, money, love—still feels they are not living a successful life. Whether it is you or not, the bottom line is that too many people are falling short of their goals, and they are puzzled as to why this is the case. So the overarching question is: Why can't I live a successful life? Why can't I reach my goals? Why is it that when I plan I either fall short of my goals or they get botched?

FEELING DISSATISFIED

Every day the world puts before us things that make us feel dissatisfied, things that make us think we have an unmet need and need

Steps To A Successful Life Today, Part 1

more. It's pathetic how we let the world trick and treat us. The world persistently says to us "You are dissatisfied. You are not living high off the hog. You need more, more, more..." And we fall for it.

A woman said, "As the bus pulled away, I realized I had left my purse under the seat. Later I called the company and was relieved that the driver had found my bag. When I went to pick it up, several off-duty bus drivers surrounded me. One man handed me my pocketbook, two typewritten pages, and a box containing the contents of my purse. 'We're required to inventory lost wallets and purses,' he explained. 'I think you'll find everything there.'"

As the lady started to put her belongings back into the pocketbook, the man continued, 'I hope you don't mind if we watch. Even though we all tried, none of us could fit everything into your purse. And we'd like to see just how you do it.'"

Every day some of us allow the world to give us a sense of discontentment, which makes us feel unfulfilled and think we need more. And we fall for it.

We don't suffer from a genetic inferiority or cultural weakness, but the world, a master craftsman, makes us feel that we don't have enough of whatever it is, so we continue to stuff things into our lives, stuff things into our purses, wallets, cabinets, closets, and garages. We lose our poise.

The world keeps saying "You have to have more, more..." and we fall for it. The world makes us feel we need the best, the new and improved, and we fall for it. And sometimes the new and improved—the best—is just one button on a new machine that we don't have on our old machine.

Filled with discontent. Always dissatisfied. The results are gluttony, unhealthy desires, and unwholesome cravings. This is not good for anyone who is trying to live a successful life. However, maybe this is not your issue. Maybe I'm not talking to you.

COMPARING OURSELVES

Maybe your problem is that you are living an unsuccessful life because you are always comparing yourself to others. Maybe you are jealous. Smart, gregarious, and energetic you are, but you have this jealous streak. You don't want to be, you don't mean to be, but you are.

Two shopkeepers were bitter rivals. Their stores were located directly across the street from each other, and they spent each day keeping track of each other's business. If one got a customer, he would smile in triumph at his rival.

One night an angel appeared to one of the shopkeepers in a dream and said, "I will give you anything you ask, but whatever you receive, your competitor will receive twice as much. Would you like to be rich? You can be very rich, but he will be twice as wealthy. Do you wish to live a long and healthy life? You can, but his life will be longer and healthier. What is your desire?"

The man frowned, thought for a moment, and then said, "Here is my request: strike me blind in one eye!"

Steps To A Successful Life Today, Part 1

Jealousy is not defunct or dead in a grave somewhere. It is still crawling around on the earth. It is still a dangerous creature. It will cause you to swing a sword at another person, but the blade will kill you; it will draw blood from you; it will bruise you for life. Has your joy been deposed, overthrown, because of jealousy? Some people have no fruits on the tree of their lives because they spend their days comparing themselves with others.

They want what others have instead of seeking what God wants for them. Instead of asking God to help them channel their emotions to be the best they can be, they are green with envy, jealous of other people's gifts, talents, and possessions. Living like this is no way to live. It is a dead-end road.

THINGS NOT GOING WELL

Let's look at one more thing that can block a successful life. Galatians 6:9 says, "Let us not grow weary in doing what is right, for we will reap at harvest time."

Some people feel they are living an unsuccessful life not only because they compare themselves to others but also because their plans are not working out. They've dug a hole, planted a seed, watered and fertilized it, but nothing has happened. For the foreseeable future, their plans are leaning and turning brown. Troubles are common to all of us, but they seem to have forgotten this. They think they are the only ones dealing with troubles.

They have forgotten that God never promised us a rose-garden life. But He did promise that we would eventually reap what we have sown. They have forgotten that with every temptation, every trial, God will provide a way out.

So when some of us pray and our troubles don't stop immediately, we figure that our lives are failures. When you don't reap immediately, and you see others reaping or getting what you feel you should have, you consider your life a failure. But this is not true, and to think this way is unwholesome. It blows away your self-confidence. So stop believing it because God didn't bring you to the earth to see you fail.

In Philippians 4:10, Paul says, "I rejoice in the Lord greatly that now at last you have revived your concern for me; indeed, you were concerned for me, but had no opportunity to show it."

And in 1 Corinthians 9:11-18 we discover that Paul was worried about being accused of preaching only for money. So what did he do? He didn't accept any.

Well, if this is so, why did he accept the Philippians' gift? Although Paul didn't accept any money at first, he maintained that it was a church's responsibility to support God's ministers. The only reason he accepted money this time was because they willingly gave it, and he was in need. Notice the text indicates that for some reason, which is not mentioned, the Philippians were not able to immediately help Paul to provide for his needs as he spread the gospel of Jesus Christ across the land.

The fact that they couldn't provide for him didn't matter. Paul kept right on spreading the gospel. He kept right on delving into the Word of God and teaching people about the love of Jesus. From empirical evidence, experience, and observation, Paul knew something: he knew how to live a successful life regardless of his circumstances or what was going on around him. When he didn't have exactly what he needed, he knew how to have a successful life anyway.

That's what God wants for you: to live a successful life regardless of what is going on in your life or around you. He wants you to have a prosperous life. He didn't create this world to conquer you. It has been His intention from the very beginning of time, from the creation of man and woman, for you to live a satisfying life, a prosperous life, a successful life. Well, what are the things you can do to have this kind of life?

ENJOYING THE MOMENT

Learn to enjoy what you have at the moment. Do you have a difficult time doing this? Well, this is difficult for a lot of people.

Several years ago I went on a mission trip that lasted a week. This is one of my vivid memories. I was away from my home, my wife, my church, my community—all that I was familiar with for one week.

All the people on this trip were much older than I. Most of them were widows. After the week was up, I was ready to go home. I thought we were going to drive straight back to Atlanta, but we didn't. Several of the ladies wanted to stop on the highway and smell the flowers, and shop in the consignment stores.

While they were doing this, I was saying to myself (because I didn't want to hurt anyone's feelings), *Will you all come on? I'm ready to get home.* I mean, we would actually stop on the highway and let people out to walk up to a fence to smell flowers or pick a flower.

We even stopped at a restaurant to eat (I didn't want to eat; I was ready to get home). The restaurant waiter said, "It will be about two hours before we can seat you." It was that crowded.

I said to myself, *Good, we can leave.* But do you know they decided to wait. I was livid. I was ready to go home. But I could have saved myself a lot of headaches if I had just enjoyed the moment. There was something beautiful being engendered in that moment: people fellowshipping together, people smelling God's beautiful flowers, people praying together. And I missed it all, my blood pressure was high, and I was upset. Why? Because I didn't enjoy the moment. I didn't enjoy the relationships in that moment. When I realized this, I knew it was time to do what Leonard Sweet says in his book *What Matters Most:* rethink relationship.

> When I consider that I am more intimately involved with two of my credit cards—American Express and Starbucks—than I am with the family that lives three doors down the street, then it is time to rethink relationships. (p.1)

Learn to enjoy the moment of relationships. But to do this, your relationships must be in proper order. Jesus said in Luke 10:27 that a proper relationship is to "Love the Lord your God with all your heart and with all your soul and with all your strength and with all your mind" and to "Love your neighbor as yourself." If you are not doing this, something will always be wrong with your relationships. If you care more about things than you do people, something is always going to be wrong with your relationships. Do what it takes to repair your relationships so that you can enjoy them. Have reasonable expectations. Focus on the good in other people. Never be too big to ask for forgiveness. And never be too angry to forgive.

Furthermore, learn to enjoy the moment of contentment. In other words, whatever that moment is, enjoy it. Paul said in Philippians 4:11-12, "I've learned by now to be quite content whatever my circumstances."

Whatever moment Paul was in—heated attacks, unpleasant surprises, deep disregard, tragic plights—he learned to let them roll off him like water on a duck's back. He learned to get the best out of the situations.

You want to live a successful life? Then learn to enjoy what you have at the moment. There is nothing wrong with having goals, in fact that is a healthy thing. But you can embrace the past and the future so tightly to your chest that your arms get too full to embrace the present. For heaven's sake, whatever the moment is enjoy it because it may not come your way again.

A minister gave his Sunday morning service as usual, but this particular Sunday it was considerably longer than normal. Later, at the door, shaking hands with the pastor, one man said, "Your sermon was simply wonderful—so invigorating and inspiring and refreshing." The minister broke out in a big smile, only to hear the man add, "Why, I felt like a new man when I woke up!"

Scores of us try to escape the moment instead of deciphering what we are supposed to receive or learn from it. Don't get so engrossed in time. A step in the direction of living a successful life is enjoying the moment, whatever is happening at that time in your life—unless it is something that is detrimental to you.

Perhaps you are saying "How do I do this? How do I enjoy the moment? I want to enjoy the moment, but I have a bad habit of sweating the small stuff, worrying about 'what if' and crowding my plate with things to do."

This is how you do it: if the waters of life are calm, enjoy it. Don't concentrate on being bored. Concentrate on the peace in that moment, the stillness in that moment, the serenity in that moment, the silence in that moment.

If bells are ringing and lights are flashing and people are dancing, giddy with excitement, enjoy that moment. Don't wish the excitement away. Don't try to escape the elation, enjoy it. Enjoy the exhilaration, enjoy the anticipation.

Not only should you enjoy the moment but also enjoy people as they are. We are each different. None of us is the same. Even people born on the same day, from the same mother, minutes apart (twins) are different. They have different handprints, different skin texture, different destinies. Paul illustrates this point well in 1 Corinthians 12:4-11:

> There are different kinds of gifts, but the same Spirit distributes them. There are different kinds of service, but the same Lord. There are different kinds of working, but in all of them and in everyone it is the same God at work.
>
> Now to each one the manifestation of the Spirit is given for the common good. To one there is given through the Spirit a message of wisdom, to another a message of knowledge by means of the same Spirit, to another faith by the same Spirit, to another gifts of healing by that one Spirit, to another miraculous powers, to another prophecy, to another distinguishing between spirits, to another speaking in different kinds of tongues, and to still another the interpretation of tongues. All these are the work of one and the same Spirit, and he distributes them to each one, just as he determines.

In the final analysis, what Paul is saying is that people are different. So don't let people's personalities get into your hair. Learn to love people as they are. Stop trying to change people. You would do better, and have far more success, with changing yourself. Noted psychologist Dr. Carl Rogers relates this point better than I can:

> I have come to believe that appreciating individuals is rather rare. I have come to think that one of the most satisfying experiences I know — and also one of

the most growth-promoting experiences for the other person—is just to fully appreciate an individual in the same way I appreciate the sunset....People are just as wonderful as sunsets—if I can let them be.

But, if I look at a sunset, as I did the other evening, I do not find myself saying, soften the orange a little on the right-hand corner, and put a bit more purple along the base, and use a little more pink in the cloud cover. I don't do that. I watch it with awe, as it unfolds. It's best when I can experience others in this way—just appreciating the unfolding of a life. Not attacking. Not criticizing. Not correcting...just appreciating others like we appreciate and enjoy the wonder, the beauty, and the uniqueness of a sunset. (James W. Moore, *Where It Hurts*, p. 45)

You can enjoy the moment by not only enjoying people but also enjoying life's challenges. Quit letting the challenges get the best of you. Enter each day with a positive attitude, expecting a blessing, and looking for things to change for the better, knowing that there will be times when things won't flow as planned.

If you get all bent out of shape (finding it difficult to keep a civil tongue) because the traffic light is holding too long, depressed because someone disturbed you while you were watching your favorite show, angry because you have junk mail, or annoyed because someone gave you an assignment you didn't expect, then the challenge is getting the best of you.

If the moment is a challenge, enjoy it too. Why? Enjoying the challenge instead of trying to escape it will help you to grow spiritually. Challenges can be daunting but need not be devastating. So let your challenges be a conduit to strengthen you. First Peter 5:8-9 says,

> Discipline yourselves; keep alert. Like a roaring lion your adversary the devil prowls around, looking for someone to devour. Resist him, steadfast in your faith, for you know that your brothers and sisters throughout the world are undergoing the same kinds of suffering.

Peter said during challenges, keep your cool. Stay alert. It stands to reason that the devil is positioning himself to get you and would like nothing better than to catch you distracted, unmindful of his presence.

Peter said keep your guard up. You're not the only one who's nose-diving into hard times. Join the club. You're not the only one who feels like when it rains it pours. It is the same with Christians everywhere. So in faith's hands, keep your hands. The challenge you are now facing won't last forever.

Someone said,

> The truth is that our finest moments are most likely to occur when we are feeling deeply uncomfortable, unhappy, or unfulfilled. For it is only in such moments, propelled by our discomfort, that we are likely to step out of our ruts and start searching for different ways or truer answers. (Unknown)

If the moment is a challenge, enjoy it too. Figure out why it is a challenge (a test, a hardship). Figure out what new opportunities or new perspectives the challenge presents to you.

I read a story recently about an interchange that took place between a dentist and his patient:

Dentist - "Try to relax. I'll pull your aching tooth in five minutes."

Patient - "How much will this cost?"

Dentist - "It'll be $100."

Patient - "That much for just five minutes' work?"

Dentist - "Well, if you prefer, I can pull it out very slowly."

Often my uncle says, "Derrick, there is more than one way to skin a cat," which means there is more than one way to do things. Ask yourself: What is the challenge? Why is it a challenge? Is there another way to tackle the challenge? Challenges will enter the doors of our lives, and if we don't know how to handle them, they can cut us down with swift, devastating strokes. Hence, the way to handle them is to enjoy the challenges rather than resent them, because they help us to mature.

After a young couple brought their new baby home, the wife suggested that her husband try his hand at changing diapers. "I'm busy," he said, "I'll do the next one."

The next time came around and she asked again. The husband looked puzzled. "Oh! I didn't mean the next diaper. I meant the next baby!"

I don't want to be a killjoy, a prophet of doom, but some of us are sourpusses. Seldom do we laugh or have fun. Almost every moment is serious. But if you want to live a successful life, you have to learn to keep things in perspective and not let everything ruffle your feathers. Learn to let go of the little things. Learn to laugh at the trivial because life is for enjoying, not getting mad over spilt milk.

Perhaps you are thinking you have been serious so long and under stress so long that you can't and don't find anything funny. But you can if you just look. Humor is everywhere.

You just have to loosen yourself from the bolt that has you screwed down and see those humorous moments. They are there. To live a successful life now, whether it is laughing or having fun, whether it is a calm moment or an exciting moment, enjoy that moment. Success often comes in moments and in what we do with those moments.

VALUES DICTATE APPETITE

Philippians 4:11 says, "Not that I am referring to being in need; for I have learned to be content with whatever I have."

The other way to live a successful life is to let your values dictate your appetite. What do I mean? I mean let your principles determine your direction; let your moral compass guide your footsteps.

Too many of us don't do this. Instead we let our appetites dictate our values, our course of action, our direction. Bottom line: we let our appetites decide how we are going to respond to life's situations and circumstances.

When actress Sophia Loren sobbed to Italian movie director Vittorio De Sica over the theft of her jewelry, he lectured her: "Listen to me, Sophia. I am much older than you, and if there is one great truth I have learned about life, it is this—never cry over anything that can't cry over you." (A.E. Hotchner, *Sophia: Living and Loving*, p.156)

Your values should point the way, not your appetites. Your appetites shouldn't turn your judgment switch on and off because when that happens 99.9 percent of the time appetites will leave the switch off. Values should guide your judgment. How do you let your values guide your judgment?

First of all, your values need to have a solid foundation. Your values need to be built on something that has worked—something that has stood the test of time.

This might sound outlandish to some: the only foundation that has stood the test of time is the Word of God. The jury is not still out on the Word of God. The Word of God is not some Jekyll and Hyde philosophy or religion, one way one day and another way the next.

No! The Word of God consistently works. So build your values, your principles, your main beliefs on that. When you have to decide what to do in any given moment, your first question is always "What would Jesus do (WWJD)?" Not what would Oprah do. Not what would mama do or daddy do or anyone else. The question is

Steps To A Successful Life Today, Part 1

"WWJD?"

Then, coupled with asking WWJD, you ask yourself what is right, just, and fair. You say to yourself "Is what I'm about to do right? Is it just? Is it fair?"

Another way you let your values direct you is this: you never do what you don't want done to you. Jesus said it like this: love your neighbor as you love yourself. Treat people like you want to be treated. Bishop T.D. Jakes points out why this is important in his book *Let It Go:*

> Though I am a Christian, I understand that many of the world's major religions shared spiritual truths that transcend time and culture and reflect a universal understanding of human natures and the seasons of one's life. Whether you call it karma, fate, destiny, or Golden Rule, I believe that one of these truths can be summed up by the adage that you reap what you sow. In the course of life, the offended and the offender will both exchange places from time to time. People who trespass on the emotional property of others' lives will someday find their own property invaded. (p. 35)

Let your values decide how you are going to respond to life's situations and circumstances. And the way you do that is to base your values on the Word of God and handle people the way you want to be handled. Give respect, love, loyalty, encouragement, care…and someday in some form these things will come back to you. Do this and success will follow you wherever you go.

THE RIGHT ATTITUDE

Someone tells of a king who was not satisfied with life. Although he was a king, he still felt unsuccessful. In fact, it was so bad he couldn't sleep, rest, or think. He called his wise men and asked them what he could do.

One very old and wise man said, "Find a man in your kingdom who is content, then wear his shirt for a day and a night, and you will be content."

That sounded like a good idea to the king, so he ordered some of his servants to search for such a person.

Days blended into weeks before his servants returned. "Well," said the king, "did you find a contented man?"

"Yes, sire," his servant replied.

"Where is his shirt?" asked the king.

"Your majesty, he didn't have one." (Stephen W. Brown, *Jumping Hurdles, Hitting Glitches, Overcoming Setbacks*, p. 162)

Feeling successful, content with your life, is not about what you have—money, stocks and bonds, land and houses. It is an attitude. Your attitude may not solve all your problems, but it will free your mind so that you can receive a lot more answers than you otherwise would.

The wrong attitude opens one door, and if the answer is not there, it stops. But the right attitude keeps looking for the answers, the way out, and eventually the right door with the right answer is opened. Jesus said it like this:

Steps To A Successful Life Today, Part 1

> Ask and it will be given to you; seek and you will find; knock and the door will be opened to you. For everyone who asks receives; he who seeks finds; and to him who knocks, the door will be opened. Which of you, if his son asks for bread, will give him a stone? Or if he asks for a fish, will give him a snake? If you, then, though you are evil, know how to give good gifts to your children, how much more will your Father in heaven give good gifts to those who ask him!

To live a successful life today, not only do you have to learn to enjoy the moment, not only do you have to let your values dictate your appetite, but also you must have the right attitude. Break you or make you, your attitude can. It can cause you to swim or sink. It can cause you to climb or fall. You having the right attitude—that's what will lead you to living a successful life.

In Philippians 4:13 you will hear these words: "I can do all things through him [Christ] who strengthens me." A person's mental attitude has an almost mind-boggling outcome on his powers, both physical and psychological. British psychiatrist J.A. Hadfield gives a noticeable illustration of this in his booklet "The Psychology of Power":

> "I asked three people," he wrote, "to submit themselves to test the effect of mental suggestion on their strength, which was measured by gripping a dynamometer." They were to grip the dynamometer with all their strength under three different sets of conditions. First he tested them under normal conditions. The average grip was 101 pounds. Then he tested

them after he had hypnotized them and told them that they were very weak. Their average grip this time was only 29 pounds! In the third test Dr. Hadfield told them under hypnosis that they were very strong. The average grip jumped to 142 pounds. (*Bits & Pieces,* May, 1991, p. 15)

To live a successful life, you must have the right attitude, and the way you do that is to do what Paul did: remind yourself daily that you are more than a conquer through Christ Jesus who strengthens you.

You will need to do this daily—build yourself up daily. If you don't you will run around this world like a chicken with its head cut off. Because as you live, doing daily what God has called you to do, life will throw you some curveballs. You have to be ready. At times you will encounter unnecessary distractions, and you cannot allow those distractions to make you feel like there is no light at the end of the tunnel.

You need a strong attitude to withstand the weight that will be put on it. So if you want to live a successful life develop your attitude muscles now. Build up your attitude now; grow your attitude now because your attitude can make you or break you. As you chart your way through this world, remember life's pressures and the treacherous waters of despair are no match for a well-developed attitude.

Anthony D'Angelo said, "Wherever you go, no matter what the weather, always bring your own sunshine." (Anthony J. D'Angelo, *The College Blue Book*) That's the kind of attitude you have to have.

Cavett Robert said, "If you don't think every day is a good day,

Steps To A Successful Life Today, Part 1

just try missing one." That's the kind of attitude you have to have.

Hubert Humphrey said, "Oh, my friend, it's not what they take away from you that counts. It's what you do with what you have left." That's the kind of attitude you have to have.

Someone else said, "Every day may not be good, but there's something good in every day." That's the kind of attitude you have to have.

To live a successful life, you have to have the right attitude.

No matter what you face, your attitude ought to be "I can do all things through Christ who strengthens me"—that's the right attitude.

- No matter what you face, your attitude ought to be "Though the trials keep coming my way I will keep on trusting Him"— that's the right attitude.
- No matter what you face, your attitude ought to be "Who shall separate us from the love of Christ? Shall trouble or hardship or persecution or famine or nakedness or danger or sword... No, in all these things we are more than conquerors through him who loved us. For I am convinced that neither death nor life, neither angels nor demons, neither the present nor the future, nor any powers, neither height nor depth, nor anything else in all creation, will be able to separate us from the love of God that is in Christ Jesus our Lord"—that's the right attitude.
- No matter what you come up against as you live this life, your attitude ought to be "God is my Refuge in the storm..."

CHAPTER ONE

Steps to a Successful Life Today, Part 2

READ SCRIPTURE: 2 Timothy 4:6-8
As for me, I am already being poured out as a libation, and the time of my departure has come. I have fought the good fight, I have finished the race, I have kept the faith. From now on there is reserved for me the crown of righteousness, which the Lord, the righteous judge, will give to me on that day, and not only to me but also to all who have longed for his appearing.

I said to you in the first part of this teaching that I don't believe anyone comes into this life saying "I want to be a loser. I don't want to accomplish a thing. I want to be left alone. I want to live and die with nothing in between. I want to live and die without having made a difference in this world." People may be uncomfortable with success, but all of us have an innate desire to succeed. Being a loser is not what we seek.

I don't believe any person is born with that kind of philosophy. If that is the case, it is deeply shocking to me. We may learn the "loser mentality" later on because of the sundry sordid episodes of life's trials and tribulations, but we are not born feeling like losers. To be cold towards life with no desire to accomplish anything good and fruitful... we are not born that way.

I have a baby granddaughter now named Sanaai. I was with her the other day, and her mother put her on a soft mat on the floor. That child was trying to crawl, trying to push up on her arms, trying to stand up.

We are sent here, born into this world with a desire to succeed no matter what our limitations are. Into this world we came with a yearning to do better and be better than we are. But some of us don't feel as if we are living a successful life. This may apply to you. Maybe you have set goals, accomplished a few of those goals, yet you feel no sense of accomplishment.

You are running the race, but for some reason you don't feel like you have crossed the finish line. There are a number of reasons why people feel this way. In the first part of this lesson, I gave you several reasons why.

You may feel that living a successful life has slipped through your fingers. But even though you feel this way—and you believe you have every reason to feel this way—feeling unsuccessful is not how God wants you to be. How do I know that? How do I know that God doesn't want you to feel unsuccessful—or be unsuccessful?

In 1 Corinthians 10:13, the Bible says, "No testing has overtaken you that is not common to everyone. God is faithful, and he will not

Steps To A Successful Life Today, Part 2

let you be tested beyond your strength, but with the testing he will also provide the way out so that you may be able to endure it." John 10:10 tells us, "The thief comes to steal and kill and destroy. I came that you might have life, and have it abundantly." In Psalm 27:1-2 we read, "The LORD is my light and my salvation; whom shall I fear? The LORD is the stronghold of my life; of whom shall I be afraid?"

God doesn't want you to feel like failure is winning. He doesn't want you to feel like failure has you pinned to the mat. To win this game called life, to have a ferocious resolve—that's what He wants for you. God wants you to have a successful life, a fruitful life, a productive life, a profitable life.

In 2 Timothy 4:7, Paul says, "I have fought the good fight, I have finished the race, I have kept the faith." Living a successful life is not like running the 40-meter dash. It is like running the Peachtree Road Race in Atlanta: perspiration, thirst, blisters, aches and pains. It's a marathon, a long run.

Paul understood this. He knew the secret of running the marathon of life. Paul says to Timothy, the person he was training for ministry, "I have lived a successful life. It wasn't easy, but I did it. I got tired along the way, but I kept running. I twisted my ankle every now and then, but I kept running. I was violently objected at times, but I kept running. I stood face-to-face with trouble and had blood-spattering battles, but I kept moving."

What I want you to notice is that when Paul writes this to Timothy, he (Paul) is about to be beheaded. He is writing from the

Mamertine Prison in Rome. This prison was awful. His cell was cold, dark, damp, and rat-infested. He had no lights, no widows, no running water, no toilet.

As he sat on that floor smelling his own urine and excrement, he was able to say with confidence that he had fought a good fight. He was able to say, "I had a quiet determination. At times I was frantically driven. I fought a good fight." Paul had finished the course. He had lived a successful life.

Paul was in a tough situation, but despite that he was clearly at peace, confident in the way he had spent his life and calmly assured as he faced death. Even in the worst circumstances imaginable, Paul knew that he was successful, victorious.

That's what God wants for us: to live a successful life, and to know we have lived a successful life. Despite what we are going through—financial difficulty, relationship problems, physical problems—God wants us to be able to say to ourselves and others that "we have fought a good fight; we have finished the race; we have kept the faith."

The question many of us are wrestling with is how do we have a successful life? Even with the whirling winds of trials and tribulations blowing in our lives, how do we live victoriously?

THERE IS MORE TO LIFE

Remember, there is more to life than what we see. This world is only one curtain that God has opened to us. There are gifts and

Steps To A Successful Life Today, Part 2

blessings behind the curtains of life that we have yet to see. Second Timothy 4:8 says, "From now on there is reserved for me the crown of righteousness, which the Lord, the righteous judge, will give to me on that day, and not only to me but also to all who have longed for his appearing."

Paul knew he was in prison, and he knew death was about to take hold of him. But as we listen to him, he is not sober or sad or miserable or morbid or depressed or cheerless. Why? Paul knew there was something beyond the relentless wave of heat of that prison he was in; although death stalked him, Paul knew there was something more to the dense, blinding fog of death that he was about to enter. He called it a reward.

For several years now, the United Methodist North Georgia Conference has held its annual conference in Athens, Georgia. Every year as we prepare for the annual conference, my wife and I pack our suitcases the night before.

The next day we get up and drive to Athens. We always take our usual route: 85 North, merge onto 285 East, then merge onto 20 West, and then we get off on Turner Hill Road and turn left at the light. As we travel, we pass through Decatur, Snellville, and a town called Between. That's right, there is a town called Between, Georgia.

Can you image someone trying to explain to someone else who's never heard of Between, Georgia, where they live? (The 2000 census said Between, Georgia, had 148 people, 61 households, and

42 families residing there.)

Remember each day that there is more to life than this world. When you die, you are going to go to heaven or hell; there is no town or city called "Between." When you breathe your last breath, you will not go to some holding tank as some religions believe. You will either go to heaven or hell.

"Lead a righteous and spiritual life," admonished a minister to a young rascal he caught causing trouble, "for there will be weeping, wailing, and gnashing of teeth among the wicked who pass on to the next world."

"What if you haven't got any teeth?" said the boy. The minister replied, "Teeth will be provided!"

This life, with the beautiful butterflies, the colorful birds flying in the wind, the breeze blowing through the trees, is not all there is. We need to remember this if we are going to live a successful life. How do we keep in mind that there is more to life than this world?

A SHORT LIFE

Every day you get up and every night you lie down to sleep, remind yourself that life is short. Life is so short the psalmist describes us as vapor. Do you realize that the only time in our lives when we like to get old is when we're kids? If you're less than ten years old, you're so excited about aging that you think in fractions. "How old are you?" "I'm four and a half." You're never thirty-six and a half ... but you're four and a half going on five!

That's the key. You get into your teens, and now they can't hold you back. You jump to the next number. How old are you? "I'm gonna be sixteen!" You could be twelve, but you're gonna be sixteen. And then the greatest day of your life happens—you become twenty-one. Even the words sound like a ceremony: twenty-one. Yes!

But then you turn thirty...ooohhh, what happened there? Makes you sound like bad milk. He turned...we had to throw him out. There's no fun now. What's wrong? What changed? You become twenty-one, you turn thirty, then you're pushing forty. Stay over there, it's all slipping away.

You become twenty-one, you turn thirty, you're pushing forty, you reach fifty...and your dreams are gone. Then you make it to sixty—you didn't think you'd make it! So you become twenty-one, you turn thirty, you're pushing forty, you reach fifty, you make it to sixty... then you build up so much speed you HIT SEVENTY!

After that, it's a day-by-day thing...you HIT Wednesday. You get into your eighties, you HIT lunch. My grandmother won't even buy green bananas—it's an investment you know, and maybe a bad one.

Every day you get up and every night you lie down to sleep, remind yourself that life is short, and that means life is transitory. You may think you have a long time to get your life in order, but you don't. As you journey through this wilderness that scrapes and bruises you, you work and play, worry and wait, entertain and love, worship and praise, but before you know it you are one step away from your finish line. Life is short. And it is even shorter when you realize you don't know when your life will end.

I hear so many people who are much older than I say, "I can't believe I am sixty [or seventy] years old now. Lord, time sure flies. Where did time go?"

USE TIME WISELY

Recently I heard someone say she got up one day, looked in the mirror, and said to herself, "Who is that old lady in the mirror?" Life is short; remind yourself of that every day. You are like a vapor.

How would you like to spend two years making phone calls to people who aren't home? Sound absurd? According to one time management study, that's how much time the average person spends trying to return calls to people who never seem to be in. Not only that, we spend six months waiting for the traffic light to turn green and another eight months reading junk mail.

These unusual statistics should cause us to do time-use evaluations. Once we recognize that simple "life maintenance" can chip away at our time in such huge blocks, we will see how vital it is that we don't busy ourselves "in vain" (Psalm 39:6).

Psalm 39:5 gives us some perspective. In David's complaint to God, he said, "You have made my days as handbreadths, and my age is as nothing before you." He meant that to an eternal God our time on earth is brief. And he doesn't want us to waste it. When we allow procrastination and idleness to become fixed parts of our persona, we throw away one of the most precious commodities God gives us: time.

Steps To A Successful Life Today, Part 2

Each minute is an irretrievable gift—and unredeemable slice of eternity. Sure, you have to make the phone calls, and you must wait at the light; you have to work; you have to maintain your household. But what about the rest of your time? Are you using it to advance the cause of Christ, to make disciples of Jesus Christ who will help transform the world? Are you using your time to enhance your relationship with God and those family members and friends whom you love? Is your time well spent? (Unknown, Daily Christian Quote)

To keep in mind that there is more to life than this world, remember not only that life is short but also remember to use the time you have wisely. After gray hairs began to color my appearance, that's when I discovered that we don't get time back.

Before every one of us is a wheel we cannot see that is spinning, and day after day it continues to turn. And day after day, humanity unsuccessfully tries to find the reverse gear. But there is no reverse gear. You can't turn the clock back.

Once that time clicks, it is gone; it cannot be put back on the clock. Once that day has shut down, it is gone; it cannot be put back on the calendar. Sometimes I find myself saying "I wish I had..." Don't let that happen to you. **Use your time wisely.** Kirbyjon H. Caldwell, pastor of Windsor Village United Methodist Church in Houston, Texas, gives us a way to use our time wisely when he says, "Ask God to use your present to help you prepare for your future."

EVALUATE YOUR LIFE

Evaluating self is also a tool you can use to remind yourself that time is short. Constantly evaluate your life and ask yourself this question: Before I die, what do I want to see happen in my life? What can I do to move towards accomplishing that objective today?

You won't pass this door again. And if you think about what you want to do while you are here—and you get it done—you shouldn't want or need to pass this way again.

Do you just want to get up in the morning, go to work, come home, eat, go to bed, and then get up to start the same routine all over again? Or do you want to complete the work God has for you? Then constantly evaluate your life.

No matter how old or young you are, there is more that God wants to do with your life. One of the persons who influenced my life was the Rev. L.A. Thompson, a United Methodist pastor. Every Easter he used to take me to Sears & Roebucks and buy me a Sunday suit. He would take me to his churches in North Carolina and let me participate in the worship service by letting me pray and read the Scripture.

When I came home from school, he fixed me lunch, and after lunch he taught me lessons about life. He taught me how to cut grass. He taught me multiplications. He taught me the importance of working hard, the importance of having a job, the importance of being frugal with my money, the importance of saving, the importance of being a good citizen. A seed of righteousness he planted in me. He not only planted it, but he watered and fertilized it.

He taught me values that would come to fruition later on in my life. If he had not crossed my path, the fruits of the Spirit that I see now would probably never have grown on the branches of my life.

There are lives God wants you to touch. There are people whose heads are in the clouds that He wants you to lift up and out so they can see the sunshine. There are people God wants to be exposed to you so they can see what they can be if they keep the faith.

Life is short. None of us has long to be here. So before this world says "time's up!" what is it that you want to do? Whose life do you want to touch? And whose life do you want to touch your life?

ACCEPT YOUR PURPOSE

In 2 Timothy 4:6, Paul says, "As for me, I am being poured out as a libation...." The word *libation* means a drink offering. It consists of wine poured out on an altar as a sacrifice to God. Its fragrance was considered pleasing to God. Paul viewed his life as an offering to God.

A boy, frustrated with all the rules he had to follow, asked his father, "Dad, how soon will I be old enough to do as I please?" The father answered immediately, "I just don't know, son. No male has ever lived that long yet."

To live a successful life, you have to do what Paul did: accept the purpose God gave you. God didn't just throw you together and then throw you out onto the stage of life and say "Do whatever you want."

You know, some people think like this. You hear of these kinds of people; they call themselves "free thinkers" or "free spirits." They believe that every human being ought to be free to do with their lives as they see fit. But listen to what Jeremiah says in Jeremiah 29:11: "For surely I know the plans I have for you, says the Lord, plans for your welfare and not for harm, to give you a future with hope."

If the free thinkers are right, that every human being has the right to think and do as he or she pleases, than what God says in Jeremiah 29:11 is a lie. And God is not a liar. The devil is a master liar, but not God. God has a plan for every one of us, and we have to find out what that plan is and live it out. How do you do that—live out God's plan for you?

The Bible tells us that God had a job for Jonah and because Jonah was disobedient—ran from his purpose—God sent a big fish to swallow him. After the fish swallowed Jonah, Jonah found himself in brutal surroundings. It must have been awful. To live out God's plan for your life, don't run from God. You just hurt yourself, frustrate yourself, upset yourself when you run.

When God has something for you to do, it is hard to run away from it. That's what David was telling us in Psalm 139:7-10 when he said,

> Where can I go from your spirit?
> Or where can I flee from your presence?
> If I ascend to heaven, you are there;

> if I make my bed in Sheol, you are there.
> If I take the wings of the morning
> and settle at the farthest limits of the sea,
> even there your hand shall lead me,
> and your right hand shall hold me fast.

God is omnipresent, which means He is everywhere. So if you go across town trying to get away from what God is calling you to do, you are still going to hear His voice. If you go to Japan or Europe or Africa trying to run from what God has called you to do, you are still going to hear God's voice.

God gave you a purpose. You are not a blank canvas. You are a picture with a story. Don't run from it; don't ignore it; don't close your eyes to it; don't disregard it. Instead, roll out the plan and follow the arrows that point the way.

The other way you live God's plan for your life is this: if you have walked away from it, stop and walk toward it. That will do a whole lot to make you stop feeling like a failure. That will do a whole lot to make you stop feeling as if your life is off course.

In John 4:34, Jesus said, "My food is to do the will of him who sent me and to complete his work." Jesus was saying "the food that keeps Me going is that I do the will of the One who sent me, finishing the work He started." To live out God's purpose for your life, stop, quit running, and do what you know He has called you to do.

If you turned your back on your purpose, then turn around and embrace your purpose now. Turn around and submit to your purpose now. Your life will be much better because of it. The grinding frustrations will diminish, the boiling dissatisfaction with your life will dissipate, and the battering unhappiness will cease hitting you so frequently. The Word of God is true! Believe it.

NEVER STOP BELIEVING

In 2 Timothy 4:7, Paul says, "I have kept the faith." Even when Paul was thrown in prison, he kept the faith. Even when the rough seas of life were rocking his boat, he kept the faith. He kept his hope in God, believing that God would work out all the things he was experiencing for his good so that whatever happened—good, bad, or indifferent—it would fertilize his faith.

You want to live a successful life? Then never stop believing that things are going to work out for you. You may be hurting inside, but don't quit. You may be under pressure, but don't quit. You may be weary, but don't quit.

You may feel that trouble has a seven inch reach advantage over you. You may feel like a 10-to-1 underdog. At times it may not look like things are going to work out, but never give up.

- Keep going to church
- Keep saying your prayers
- Keep going to Bible study
- Keep working in the church

God didn't create you to be defeated. He didn't create you to be a loser. If He did that, He wouldn't be a loving God. He put you together to be able to say what Paul said in our text: "I have fought the good fight, I have finished the race, I have kept the faith."

God put you together not to fail the test but to pass the test, not to lose the battle but to win the battle. To live a successful life, you have to keep on fighting, keep on pushing forward, keep on trying.

CHAPTER TWO

Steps to a Successful Life Today, Part 3

READ SCRIPTURE: Genesis 1:28-31
God blessed them, and God said to them, 'Be fruitful and multiply, and fill the earth and subdue it; and have dominion over the fish of the sea and over the birds of the air and over every living thing that moves upon the earth.' God said, 'See, I have given you every plant yielding seed that is upon the face of all the earth, and every tree with seed in its fruit; you shall have them for food. And to every beast of the earth, and to every bird of the air, and to everything that creeps on the earth, everything that has the breath of life, I have given every green plant for food.' And it was so. God saw everything that he had made, and indeed, it was very good. And there was evening and there was morning, the sixth day.

As I read the Word of God, I have no doubt about it. As I read from Genesis to Revelation, I have found nothing that would make me believe otherwise. God did not put us here for the world to conquer us. God did not create us in His image for life to defeat us. After God made us, breathed the breath of life into us,

Steps To A Successful Life Today, Part 3

and molded us, He did not place us in our specific locations for the world to put a death hold on us and beat us into submission. This was never His plan.

Genesis 1:28 says, "God blessed them, and God said to them, 'Be fruitful and multiply, and fill the earth and subdue it; and have dominion over the fish of the sea and over the birds of the air and over every living thing that moves upon the earth.'"

Circle the word "fruitful." Circle the word "multiply." Circle the phrase "fill the earth." Circle the phrase "subdue it." Circle the phrase "have dominion over." From the beginning of time, God meant for us to live a successful life, a prosperous life, a fruitful life. God wants us to succeed. He wants us to live a successful life. Physically, mentally, spiritually, emotionally, and financially, He wants our cups to overflow. Well, how do we make this happen? How do we have a successful life?

To live a successful life, you have to be responsible for what you have been given. In Genesis 1:28, God said to Adam and Eve "rule over." When God said "have dominion over" and "rule over," He was telling them to take responsibility for things He had given them. In other words, He was telling them to be responsible individuals. You have to be a responsible person if you want to live a successful life. Let me tell you how you do this: do what you say you are going to do. Don't make promises that you are not going to keep.

Don't be careless with the things God has given you. He has given you a family. He has given you gifts. He has given you material things.

He has given you a church home. And you can't be careless with any of them. How do you expect God to bless you with more responsibilities when you are careless with the responsibilities you have? How do you expect God to bless you with more blessings when you are lackadaisical and foolish with the blessings He has already given you?

Not only should you not be careless with the things God has already given you, but you should also stop making excuses. George Washington Carver profoundly said, "Ninety-nine percent of all failures come from people who have a habit of making excuses" (www. LeadershipNow). Some of us can't seem to stop saying

- "I would but... "
- "I want to but..."
- I was getting ready to but...

Anytime you make one of these statements, you are making an excuse. You are being an irresponsible individual. When God told Adam and Eve to take "dominion over" the earth, He was telling them to be responsible individuals. That is one of the key ingredients to living a successful life.

WISDOM

There is something else we need to know about living a successful life. James 1:5 says, "If any of you is lacking in wisdom, ask God, who gives to all generously and ungrudgingly, and it will be given you." To live a successful life, add wisdom to your life's toolbox.

What is wisdom? Wisdom is knowledge guided by understanding. So if you have knowledge and you don't have understanding then you don't have wisdom. To live a successful life, add wisdom to your life; get knowledge but also get understanding. Why? You need wisdom to help you settle down and see life from God's perspective. God looks at things from a different perspective than we do. And however God sees things is how it ought to be; it's the best way.

You may see a trial you are going through as punishment, something that is setting you back. But God may see the trial as a test of your faith to produce endurance that will help you to mature in your spiritual walk. Wisdom helps you to see things as God sees them.

You need wisdom not only to see things from God's perspective but also to help you make the right choices in life. In this life, the world will say to you "live and let live; spend and don't worry about anything; live high on the hog, and worry about paying for it later." But wisdom says if you buy that you are going to have to pay for it, and you know you don't have the money for that right now—so put it back.

This world will tell you to do whatever works for you, even if it means being selfish, even if it means hurting someone. But wisdom says love your neighbor as you love yourself. The world says worry about this and worry about that, which drives you to shake in your boots. But wisdom says do not worry about tomorrow, for tomorrow will bring worries of its own. Today's trouble is enough for today.

Living A Successful Life Today

You need wisdom to make the right choices.

The text says, "If any of you is lacking in wisdom, ask God...." You can have all the knowledge in the world, all the degrees in the world, all the intelligence in the world, but to know how to use that knowledge for your highest good you need wisdom. Short and sweet: you need knowledge guided by understanding.

There's a little fellow named Junior who would hang out at the local grocery store. The manager didn't know what Junior's problem was, but the boys liked to tease him. They said he was two bricks short of a load, or two pickles shy of a barrel. To prove it, sometimes the boys offered Junior his choice between a nickel and a dime. He always took the nickel, and the other boys would tease him. They said, "He chooses the nickel instead of the dime because the nickel is bigger."

One day after Junior grabbed the nickel, the store manager got fed up with the boys tricking Junior. So he got on the warpath and pulled Junior off to one side and said, "Junior, those boys are making fun of you. They think you don't know the dime is worth more than the nickel. Are you grabbing the nickel because it's bigger, or what?"

Junior said, "Well, if I took the dime, they'd quit doing it!"

When you have wisdom, you make smart decisions. You make decisions that don't hinder you but help you. There may be several choices to make, but you make the choices that are going to be positive outcomes for you, the choices that are going to make things better for you and not worse. Wisdom helps you to get to the best conclusion for you. Where does wisdom come from, and how do you get it?

James 1:5 says, "If any of you lacks wisdom, he should ask God." Where does wisdom come from? God. Not from how old you are (there are some old fools because they didn't learn from experience). Wisdom comes not from being smart, not from your status in life, but from God who designed this universe, taught the mockingbird to sing, and hung the stars, moon, and sun in the sky.

How do you get wisdom? You ask God. You say to Him, "Lord, I need wisdom. I have a choice to make, a problem to solve, so help me to make the wisest choice." Ask. That's how you get wisdom. Where else does wisdom come from? Is there another place where we can gain wisdom?

It can come from experience if you let it. Listen to what these children say and I think you will understand what I mean:

Patrick, age ten, said, "Never trust a dog to watch your food." I wonder how he knows that.

- Michael, fourteen, said, "When your dad is mad and asks you, 'Do I look stupid?' don't answer him." I wonder how he knows that.

- Michael also said, "Never tell your mom her diet's not working."

- Randy, age nine, said, "Stay away from prunes." One wonders how he discovered that bit of wisdom.

- Karen, age nine, said, "Never hold a dust buster and a cat at the same time."

- Naomi, age fifteen, said, "If you want a kitten, start out by asking for a horse."

- Lauren, age nine, said, "Felt markers are not good to use as lipstick."

- Joel, age ten, said, "Don't pick on your sister when she's holding a baseball bat."

- Eileen, age eight, said, "Never try to baptize a cat."

Wisdom can come from God, but it can also come from experience. Whenever you go through trials, make the wrong choice, or do the wrong thing, don't sink into despair and stay there. Don't let the experience drive you out of control. Instead learn from the experience—gain wisdom from it.

Wisdom can come from experience. Examples: if you do the wrong thing and then start doing it right, you have gained wisdom. If you take the wrong turn in life and turn around and take the

Steps To A Successful Life Today, Part 3

right turn, you have gained wisdom.

From experience wisdom can come. From a bad encounter in your life wisdom can come. Sometimes going through a trial can mature you and give you the ability to use the lessons you gained in the trial for your highest good, if you let it.

CONTROL YOUR EMOTIONS

The book of James is an interest book. Some have said this book was written in response to antinomianism, an extreme view of Paul's teachings about faith. In this book, James outlines what it takes to walk by faith.

In James 1:19-20, we see something else that we need to know about living a successful life: "You must understand this, my beloved: let everyone be quick to listen, slow to speak, slow to anger; for your anger does not produce God's righteousness." You live a successful life by not allowing your emotions to control you.

In the book *Extremely Loud and Incredibly Close* by Jonathan Safran Foer, the character Oskar articulates so well why controlling our emotions is vital to living a successful life as he talks to his therapist, Dr. Fein:

> "I feel too much. That's what's going on." "Do you think one can feel too much? Or just feel in the wrong ways?" "My insides don't match up with my outsides." "Do anyone's insides and outsides match up?"

"I don't know. I'm only me." "Maybe that's what a person's personality is: the difference between the inside and outside." "But it's worse for me." "I wonder if everyone thinks it's worse for him." "Probably. But it really is worse for me." (Jonathan Safran Foer, *Extremely Loud and Incredibly Close*, p. 201)

When you let your emotions control you, you become confused. You blow hot and cold, uncertain about who you are, what you should be doing, and what you should stand for. Furthermore, when you let your emotions control you, you do things without thinking. When your emotions control you, you also say things without thinking.

A retired man who volunteers to entertain patients in nursing homes and hospitals went to one local hospital in Brooklyn and took his portable keyboard along. He told some jokes and sang some funny songs at patients' bedsides. When he finished he said, in farewell, "I hope you get better."

One elderly gentleman replied, "I hope you get better too."

When your emotions control you, you say things without thinking—hurtful things, things which could have been said a little better or more gently. Some of us let our emotions control us, which boggles our minds and bogs us down and contributes to our lack of living a successful life.

There are multitudes of ways your feelings can control you. Scientists have taken all those emotions and put them in these basic classifications: joy, acceptance, fear, surprise, sadness, disgust, anger, and anticipation. You should not let any of these emotions have power over you. I am not saying repress or ignore your feelings. When you do that, you will be sitting on a powder keg; your emotions could explode and cause you huge problems. What I am saying is learn to manage your emotions, manage your attitude.

When you get angry and react the same way every time, when you get disgusted and frustrated and react the same way every time, do you know what this says about you? That your emotions are controlling you and you are not controlling your emotions. Let's look at some steps to help you break loose from the tentacles of your emotions.

The first thing is this: don't jump to conclusions. I remember several years ago, while I was sitting in my grandmother's living room, a cousin came to me, sat down beside me, and said, "I know my wife told you that I came in late last night. And that I have been drinking a lot. And that I have my license revoked and I'm not supposed to be drinking at all."

I replied, "What makes you assume that?" He responded, "I could tell by the way you were looking at me that my wife told you." And I looked at him and said, "I didn't know any of those things until you just told me. Your wife hasn't told me anything."

When you jump to conclusions, you immediately assume the worst. You think people know things they don't know. You get paranoid, unreasonable, and suspicious. So don't jump to conclusions. Get the facts first before you respond, because if you don't you are going to look foolish. You are going to assume people know something that they don't know.

Second, you learn to control your emotions by asking yourself these questions:

- How would God want me to respond?
- What do I want the outcome to be from this situation?
- What response would make me proud?
- What is another way I can look at this situation or event in my life that is causing me to feel this way?

Your emotions control you when you believe there is only one way you can respond. This kind of thinking will cause you to skate on thin ice. There is always more than one way to respond to a situation or event in your life. Furthermore, you cannot control all the events that happen in your life, but you can control your response (your reaction, your comeback), and by doing that you will be mastering your attitude rather than it mastering you. To live a successful life, learn to control your emotions, your passions, your feelings.

Feelings are much like waves, we can't stop them from coming but we can choose which one to surf. (Jonatan Mårtensson)

BUILD SELF-CONFIDENCE

Genesis 1:28 says "he blessed them." God not only gave Adam and Eve authority and responsibilities, "he blessed them." Isn't that a good phrase? That's something to hold onto—that's something to circle in your Bible, "he blessed them." That's something that can build up your confidence as you live this life: "he blessed them." When I get depressed I turn to this phrase, and it helps simmer me down and build my confidence. To live a successful life, not only do you need to control your emotions, you also need to build up your self-confidence.

People who have problems with self-confidence have a difficult time setting goals, writing those goals down, and achieving them. Self-confidence is a vital part of living a successful life; it is a vital part of getting others to believe in you. If you got on a plane and noticed the pilot was frantic, sweating on his forehead and wringing his hands, would you want him to fly the plane? I wouldn't.

If you don't believe in yourself, no one else will. If you don't believe that you can, you are defeating yourself, not someone else. Many of us lack self-confidence, and as children of God this should not be the case. You ought to have self-confidence because just as God blessed Adam and Eve, He blessed you too. You say how did He bless you?

He blessed you with Jesus. He blessed all of us with Jesus. There are several reasons why I follow Jesus. He is my bread and butter. He died for me. He gave me a new life. He gave me eternal life, meaning when my physical body decays my relationship with God doesn't cease because according to Romans 8 nothing can separate me from the love of God that is in Christ Jesus.

Another reason I follow Jesus is that He Himself had self-confidence. When I picture Jesus, I see Him humble but with His head held high; I see Him speaking clearly; I see Him looking His problems in the eye and saying "I may be pushed on every side, but I am not crushed; perplexed, but not in despair; persecuted, but not abandoned; struck, but not destroyed" (2 Corinthians 4:8-9).

Self-confidence is a vital part of life. If Jesus had it, I know we have to have it too. "I tell you the truth," Jesus said in John 14:12, "anyone who has faith in me will do what I have been doing. He will do even greater things than these, because I am going to the Father."

Self-confidence affects how people see you. It affects your behavior, your body language, your speech, your demeanor, your interaction with people, your successes and failures. It is an important part of living a successful life. Let me be more specific.

When you are self-confident, you will do what is right, even if it means people will criticize and tease you for doing it. When you are self-confident, you are willing to take risk, willing to try what seems to be impossible, willing to go the extra mile. When you are not self-confident this is what happens: you go along with the crowd, even when you know it is wrong. You stay in your comfort zone; you do what you have always done.

Low self-confidence can cause you to be your own worst enemy. That's why to live a successful life you have to build, develop, grow your self-confidence. How do you do this?

You have to defeat the negative thoughts. You have to keep

Steps To A Successful Life Today, Part 3

negative people out of your life. In other words, you have to speak up; you have to speak your mind and manage the negative things and people who will come your way and not allow them to manage you.

You see, negative thoughts and negative people can depress you. They can suck all your positive energy out. But if you are going to live a successful life, you can't allow this to happen. You have to fight back. You say how?

Remember every day that God blessed you, and He blessed you with Jesus. He sent Jesus to stand behind you so that you could live a successful life. He sent Jesus to help you be an overcomer—victorious. He blessed you. That's why you ought to be self-confident—because no matter what you face you have Jesus to face it with you.

No matter what obstacles come your way, no matter what storm comes your way, no matter what heartache comes your way, you have Jesus. And that means you are not alone. That means "you can do all things through Christ who strengthens you" (Philippians 4:13).

CHAPTER THREE

Reigniting Your Passion for God, Part 1

READ SCRIPTURE: Mark 12:28-34
One of the scribes came near and heard them disputing with one another, and seeing that he answered them well, he asked him, 'Which commandment is the first of all?' Jesus answered, 'The first is, "Hear, O Israel: the Lord our God, the Lord is one; you shall love the Lord your God with all your heart, and with all your soul, and with all your mind, and with all your strength." The second is this, "You shall love your neighbour as yourself." There is no other commandment greater than these.' Then the scribe said to him, 'You are right, Teacher; you have truly said that "he is one, and besides him there is no other"; and "to love him with all the heart, and with all the understanding, and with all the strength", and "to love one's neighbour as oneself", — this is much more important than all whole burnt-offerings and sacrifices.' When Jesus saw that he answered wisely, he said to him, 'You are not far from the kingdom of God.' After that no one dared to ask him any question.

Whatever happened to some people's passion for God? Where is that zeal, that fire, that enthusiasm? A Sunday school teacher asked the children just before she dismissed them, "And why is it necessary to be quiet in church?" Little Johnny jumped up and yelled, "Because people are sleeping!"

Whatever happened to some people's passion for God? Where is that zeal, that fire, that enthusiasm? Maybe you have lost your passion for God. You started out on fire for the Lord but then your fire went out.

Maybe this is not you. Maybe your problem is this: you discovered your gift, started using your gift, and then for some reason you disappeared from the church; oh, you might go every now and then—on special days. But that's about it.

No? That's not you? Maybe this is you: God performed a miracle in your life; you got excited, came to the pastor and said you were going to do this, that, and the other for the church, and you started off doing it, but then something happened (the pastor doesn't know and no one else does either) and you just quit. Why? Why do people lose their passion for God?

Some of us have lost our passion for God because we prayed and felt we didn't get an answer or we didn't get the answer we wanted. And not getting the answer we wanted took something out of us. It zapped our energy and our focus.

Three priests were sitting around discussing how things were going at their respective parishes. The first priest complained of a terrible bat infestation at his church, and it was soon apparent that this was something of an epidemic at all three parishes. After much discussion of all matters clerical, they went home for the night. After a week or so, they met again and discussed the bat problem:

- Priest 1: "I tried to get rid of my bats this week. I shot at them with my shotgun, but I think I damaged the belfry more than the bats! I still have no way of getting rid of them."
- Priest 2: "I tried another way. I couldn't bring myself to shoot them; after all they are God's creatures, so I went up with a big box. I knocked all the bats into the box with a stick and drove out to the forest where I released them. But they were back at the church before I was!"
- Priest 3: "I've solved the problem. I did much the same thing. I had all the bats in the box, but before I released them I baptized and confirmed every one of them, and they have not been back since."

Some people have lost their passion for God not only because they didn't get an answer to their prayers but also because they were never really on fire for the Lord. All they did was get baptized and confirmed; they were never really on fire. They never really had passion for God. They never really had fervor for God. When you came to God or took on the task you said you were going to do, was it a head response instead of a heart response?

And then there are others who don't have a passion for God because they think they are doing the church and the pastor a favor when they do something in the church. I cannot tell you the number of people who have said to me, "Reverend, we are going to help you be successful at this church." I don't say anything; I just scratch my head, look at them, and say to myself, *You are going to help me do what?*

The church is not about the preacher; it is supposed to be about God, spreading His love, spreading His message, spreading His mercy and grace across the earth. So it is not about helping the preacher be successful; it is about you doing your part to help further the kingdom of God, and that my friend helps you not the preacher.

Several years ago I heard a story about a woman who died and went to heaven. After arriving in heaven, the angels gave her a pair of wings and asked her and others to follow them as they took them to their new residences. The first stop was a huge mansion with acres of land. But this was not the woman's new residence; it was someone else's.

They went to several places and all of them were magnificent. But none of them were the woman's. After about seven stops they came to a little shack with a broken-down door and broken windows. The angel looked at the woman and said, "This is your place, your new residence." The woman said furiously, "How come I get a shack and everyone else got a mansion?" The angel replied, "From the timber you sent us from the work you did on the earth, this was all we could build."

Doing your part to further the kingdom of God helps you. It is about you being a blessing so one day you can be blessed beyond your

Living A Successful Life Today

wildest imagination. Jesus clearly illustrated this point in the story He told about the owner who gave talents (money) to three men.

Jesus said an owner went on a long trip, and he needed his servants to care for his finances. He gave the first servant $5000, the second $2000, and the third $1000. The men who had $5000 and $2000 went and invested the money and made more. The one who was given $1000 buried his money in the ground instead of investing it; of course, he didn't make any money.

Soon the owner returned to receive a report from the men about what they had done with the owner's property. The man who had $5000 showed the owner that he had increased what he was given, and the owner was pleased and said to him, "Well done, good and faithful servant! You have been faithful with a few things; I will put you in charge of many more. Come and share my happiness!"

The owner did the same thing to the second man because he too had increased what he was given. But the man who had buried the money he was given and didn't increase it disappointed the owner. The owner said to him, "You are lazy and wicked." He took the $1000 from the man and gave it to the other two men; he condemned the lazy man because he had not used well the money given to him.

The work you do down here won't save you, but it will determine what you get when you get to heaven. So the work you do is about God, and it also has to do with you. It is not about the Methodist Church, the Baptist Church, the Catholic Church. It is not about the pastor; it is not about your home church; it is about God

Reigniting Your Passion For God, Part 1

and you. Your labor will determine your reward in heaven.

But some people don't understand this, so when something bad happens to them—they are wounded, upset, disenchanted. They lose their passion for God, not understanding that losing their passion will have even greater consequences.

Don't let anything steal your passion for God. Being disappointed, dissatisfied, or disenchanted will sometimes invade your life, but that's no reason to let one of the most important things you have be taken from you.

In Mark 12:28-33, Mark gives you four other reasons you should never allow your passion for God to be taken from you.

First of all, that is what Jesus told us to do. Mark said that one day as Jesus was traveling the religious leaders asked Him about several things. One of those questions had to do with what is the greatest commandment. You see, during that time the Jewish leaders had accumulated hundreds of laws—613 by one historian's count.

Some religious leaders tried to distinguish between major and minor laws, and some taught that all the laws were equally binding and that it was dangerous to make any distinction. But one of the religion scholars came up, hearing the lively exchanges of question and answer, and decided to see what Jesus had to say about the laws, so he asked this question: "Jesus, which is most important of all the commandments?"

Jesus replied, "The first in importance is, 'Listen, Israel: The Lord your God is one; so love the Lord God with all your passion

Living A Successful Life Today

and prayer and intelligence and energy.' And here is the second: 'Love others as well as you love yourself.' There is no other commandment that ranks with these." (NIV Bible Commentary)

Did you hear that? Passion. That's one of the keys to living a successful life today: having passion for God, loving Him with all your heart. Having passion for God is not something the church made up. Having passion for God is something Jesus taught the early church, and it is something He wants the twenty-first-century church to practice too.

Second, without a passion for God, you will not be excited about the work of the church: feeding the hungry, clothing the naked, making disciples, spreading the love of Jesus, making a difference in the world.

Third, without passion for God, we do what some of us are doing now: we're lazy about our commitment to the church; we don't pray as we should; we don't tithe as we should or give offerings as we should; we make promises to God and the church that we don't keep.

Fourth, without passion for God, you may hear the voice of God telling you to do something, but you will not be mobilized, moved, motivated to get it done. So if you have lost your passion, get busy reigniting it. Reigniting your passion for God is another step in the direction of living a successful life. How do you reignite your passion for God?

NOURISH YOUR SPIRIT

To reignite your passion for God, you have to begin to nourish your spirit. This nourishing your spirit every once in a while is not going to do it. This nourishing your spirit two Sundays out of the month, or on special days—Mother's Day, Father's Day, Easter, Christmas, church anniversary—won't do it.

My wife had some plants, and in the process of her moving from one school to another we forgot to water them. Do you know what happened? They withered and died. Your spirit is just like that plant. If you don't water your spirit with the Word of God on a regular basis, your spirit will wither; it will dry up and waste away. And when that happens you lose your passion for God. So if you want to reignite your passion for God, you have to nourish your spirit. Let me give you some ways to do this.

To nourish your spirit, learn to love yourself. Too many of us set out to love other people when we don't love ourselves. Don't you know it is difficult to love someone else when you don't love yourself? Don't you know it is difficult to care for other people when you don't care for yourself?

Mark 12:31 says, "You shall love your neighbour as yourself." Someone said, "What you think of yourself is much more important than what others think of you." If your love for yourself is improper, you can't properly love anyone else. If you don't know how to look out for your best interest, you can't look out for someone else's.

You love other people to the degree that you love yourself. If your love for yourself is unhealthy, you are going to have an unhealthy love for God. You want to reignite your passion for God? Then nourish your spirit by learning to love yourself. Care for yourself.

There is someone who is very close to me. The last time I went home I went to see him. When I got there, he had not come home yet, so his wife and I talked. She told me that he had been having fainting spells and blood in his stool.

After about forty-five minutes my friend walked through the door. We greeted each other with a hand grip and a hug, and afterwards we sat down and had a long talk. He was just as I remembered him—loquacious. When I managed to get a word in, I told him that his wife informed me about his fainting spells and blood in his stool.

I asked him if he had gone to the doctor. He said "not yet." I asked him if he had made an appointment. And he said "not yet." I said, "Well, I understand this has been going on for a month." He said he was going to make an appointment soon.

Now, I want you to know that the same way he treats himself—carefree, unconcerned, with disregard—is the same way he treats his family, the same way he treats his wife and children and friends. Could you be in deep water because you don't know how to love yourself?

Learn to care for yourself because if you don't, you can't properly care for anyone else. You can't do right by anyone else. You can't love God with passion if you don't love yourself with passion. Nourish your spirit by loving yourself. And once you can do that properly, you can love God properly; you can love Him with passion. This on-and-off relationship you have with God—here today and gone tomorrow—will cease when you learn to love you.

You nourish your spirit by not only learning to love yourself but also feeding on spiritual food. What spiritual food do you have available to you? Psalm 119:105 says, "Your word is a lamp to my feet and a light to my path." Matthew 4:3-4 says, "The tempter came and said to him, 'If you are the Son of God, command these stones to become loaves of bread.' But he answered, 'It is written, One does not live by bread alone, but by every word that comes from the mouth of God.'"

John Wesley said, "I am a creature of a day. I am a spirit come from God, and returning to God. I want to know one thing: the way to heaven. God himself has condescended to teach me the way. He has written it down in a book. Oh, give me that book! At any price give me the book of God. Let me be a man of one book." (John Wesley, *Sermons on Several Occasions: Volume 1*, Preface)

One of the most important spiritual foods you have available to you is the Word of God. You can read health books, journals, and magazines, but none of these will feed your soul like the Word of God. In due time, all these other resources will fail, but not the Word of God.

When I was a Boy Scout and later on a Marine, if we went out at night, one of the most important pieces of equipment I had was my flashlight. Without it we could not see at night. Without it we stood a strong possibility of walking into trees, falling into a hole, or stepping on a snake. As you walk through life's jungles, you need a flashlight, which is the Word of God, to guide you, because without it your chances of making it through will be difficult.

And so you need the Word to nourish your spirit, to show you the way, and when you realize this—really realize this—your passion for God will be reignited. You will want to know more about Him, draw closer to Him, and love Him with all your heart, with all your soul, and with all your strength.

ACCORDING TO HIS WILL

The Bible tells us that Abraham and Sarah wanted a child, and God had promised to give them a child. But years traveled by and Sarah still had not given birth. The child that God promised them did not come according to Abraham and Sarah's timetable.

To reignite your passion for God, come to grips with the fact that God is not going to give you everything you think you ought to have when you think you ought to have it. Don't let this go in one ear and out the other. God is not going to bring everything you want into fruition based on your time. Perhaps you are saying "But the Bible says knock and the door will be opened to you...seek and you will find...." That doesn't mean He is going to give you everything you pray for. Why, you say? Why is God not going to give me everything I pray for?

God is not going to give you everything you pray for because it may not be in line with His will for you. First John 5:14 says, "And this is the boldness we have in him, that if we ask anything according to his will, he hears us." The key phrase in this verse is "according to his will." When you ask God for something don't forget this: "according to his will."

There are people who have walked away from the church or walked away from a task or job or relationship or ministry because God didn't give them what they asked for. Please hear this. And I may be stepping into your backyard. But you need to hear this: God doesn't work that way; I don't care what the prosperity gospel says. You can name and claim it all you want, but if what you are naming and claiming is not in line with God's will for you, it is not going to happen.

There are certain things God has for you that He is not going to give me. Why? Because that is what He has for you. There are certain things God has for me that He is not going to give to you. Why? Because that is what He has for me. You can huff and puff and get bent out of shape all you want, but if it isn't in line with God's will for you, you can blow the house down if you want but that will not move God to give it to you.

A few days ago I was in a store when a teenage boy came up to the checkout counter, raised some type of game in his mother's face, and said, "Mom, can I get this? She said, "No."

But that didn't stop that boy from asking. Again he said, "Mom, can I get this? I don't understand why I can't get this." And his mother turned and looked him straight in the eyes and said,

Living A Successful Life Today

"Because I said no."

The bottom line is this: sometimes God's answer is no. When you understand this, it will help you refrain from getting upset with God and the church; it will help you not lose your passion for God. When He says no to you, it doesn't mean He doesn't love you. It just means that what you are asking for is not for you. It just means that if God gives you what you are asking for, He knows it would leave you in ruins; it would send your life in a tailspin. You know what this ought to say to you? That God has your back. That He is always going to do what is best for you, even if you don't think so.

One of the ways to reignite your passion is to understand that God is not going to give you everything you ask for. Why? He has your back, meaning He knows what is best for you.

Sometimes God's answer is "Yes, but not now." You want it now, but God says "not now." Some people want God to jump when they say jump, do when they say do, move when they say move. But let me say it again: God doesn't work like that. He moves when He gets ready. He moves when He knows the time is right.

Sometimes the time is not right for what you are requesting. God may be saying "Okay, you can have that or I will grant that. But you are going to have to be patient. There are some things I have to fix, put in place, get right before what you want can take place."

So the lesson to learn is this: God knows something that you don't know. "Yes, you can have it but not now."

Another reason that God will not give you everything you ask for is that it may do you more harm than good. Romans 11:33-36 says,

> O the depth of the riches and wisdom and knowledge of God! How unsearchable are his judgments and how inscrutable his ways! 'For who has known the mind of the Lord? Or who has been his counselor?' 'Or who has given a gift to him, to receive a gift in return?' For from him and through him and to him are all things. To him be the glory for ever. Amen.

Listen to this same verse from *The Message* translation:

> Have you ever come on anything quite like this extravagant generosity of God, this deep, deep wisdom? It's way over our heads. We'll never figure it out. Is there anyone around who can explain God? Anyone smart enough to tell him what to do? Anyone who has done him such a huge favor that God has to ask his advice?

> Everything comes from him; Everything happens through him; Everything ends up in him. Always glory! Always praise!
> Yes. Yes. Yes.

God can see what you can't see, and He knows what you don't know. He knows whether answering your prayer will hurt you or help you. He knows whether answering your prayer will burden you or bless you. So quit getting mad with God when you don't get your way. Quit getting worked up with the church when you don't get your way. Quit getting peeved with the pastor when you don't get your way.

When you understand that God is not going to grant all your requests, give you everything you ask for, you will be better off. You will regain your passion for God because you realize that God has your back. He is your best friend. He has your best interest at heart, and He is always looking out for you. And whatever He doesn't allow, it is for a good reason. And whatever He does allow, it is for a good reason. We don't know what it is, but God does.

I remember years ago when I was in college, I lost my passion for God. I lost my passion for the church, and I walked away. I got fed up with the church. Why? Because I prayed for something that God didn't grant, He didn't give me. A couple years later I realized why. You see, if He had given me what I asked for, it would have destroyed my life. It would have made me miserable, and I never would have accepted my call to ministry.

When I realized what God had done, I asked for forgiveness for my selfish ways. I went back to the church, accepted my call, and fell in love with God all over again. Why? I realized that no matter how it looked, God had my back. I realized that He is my best friend.

When pressures are doing their best to crush you, He has your back. When circumstances are doing their best to frustrate you, tear you down, pull you into darkness, He has your back. Nobody is concerned about you like He is concerned. Nobody cares about you like He does. No matter how it looks God is present. So the winning edge for you is no matter what comes up, continue to love the Lord with all your soul, with all your mind, and with all your strength. God has your back.

CHAPTER FOUR

Reigniting Your Passion for God, Part 2

―――⦅∞⦆―――

READ THE SCRIPTURE: Psalm 42

As a deer longs for flowing streams,
    so my soul longs for you, O God.

My soul thirsts for God,
    for the living God.
When shall I come and behold
    the face of God?
My tears have been my food
    day and night,
while people say to me continually,
    'Where is your God?'
These things I remember,
    as I pour out my soul:
how I went with the throng,
    and led them in procession to the house of God,
with glad shouts and songs of thanksgiving,
    a multitude keeping festival.
Why are you cast down, O my soul,
    and why are you disquieted within me?
Hope in God; for I shall again praise him,
    my help and my God.
My soul is cast down within me;

> therefore I remember you
> from the land of Jordan and of Hermon,
> > from Mount Mizar.
> Deep calls to deep
> > at the thunder of your cataracts;
> all your waves and your billows
> > have gone over me.
> By day the LORD commands his steadfast love,
> > and at night his song is with me,
> > a prayer to the God of my life.
> I say to God, my rock,
> > 'Why have you forgotten me?
> Why must I walk about mournfully
> > because the enemy oppresses me?'
> As with a deadly wound in my body,
> > my adversaries taunt me,
> while they say to me continually,
> > 'Where is your God?'
> Why are you cast down, O my soul,
> > and why are you disquieted within me?
> Hope in God; for I shall again praise him,
> > my help and my God.

Where is that energy you used to have for the Lord? What happened to that fire that was in your heart for Jesus?

A minister dies and, resplendent in his clerical collar and colorful robes, waits in line at the Pearly Gates. Just ahead of him is a guy dressed in sunglasses, a loud shirt, leather jacket, and jeans.

Saint Peter addresses this guy saying, "Who are you so that I may know whether or not to admit you to the kingdom of heaven?" The guy replies, "I'm Joe Green, taxi driver, of Noo Yawk City."

Saint Peter consults his list, smiles, and says to the taxi driver,

"Take this silken robe and golden staff, and enter into the kingdom." So the cab driver enters heaven with his robe and staff, and the minister is next in line. He stands erect.

Without being asked, he proclaims, "I am Joseph Snow, head pastor of Saint Mary's for the last forty-three years." Saint Peter consults his list and says, "Take this cotton robe and wooden staff and enter the kingdom of heaven."

The minister says, "Just a minute. That man was a taxi driver and you issued him a silken robe and golden staff. But I get wood and cotton. How can this be?" Saint Peter says, "Up here, we go by results. While you preached, people slept; while he drove, people prayed."

Where is that energy you used to have for the Lord? What happened to that fire that was in your heart for Jesus? There was a time when you couldn't keep some of us away from the church. There was a time when we would throw down for Jesus. If there was a church service, a revival, a choir concert, a task to be done for the church, we were the first to be there. But now our wick is wet. Our fire for the Lord has gone out.

A PERSON HURT THEM

Some people lose their passion because someone hurt them. They attended church faithfully but then something happened. A conflict arose in their lives. A friend or spouse disappointed them. That disappointment led to an ill nature: anger. And that anger led to a spiritual crisis. And that spiritual crisis led to quitting the church.

A PASTOR HURT THEM

Several years ago I had a layperson in the church who would always fight me, not physically, but she fought whatever idea I had. One day I got fed up with it and decided to confront her, so I asked her to come to my office so we could talk.

After she arrived, I asked her to have a seat. I said to her, "Mrs._____, why are you always fighting me? I don't understood what is going on between us. You and I have never had an argument. So I don't understand why you are my enemy. Did I do something to hurt your feelings?"

She replied, "No, Reverend, you didn't do anything to hurt me. The pain I have came from another pastor. He really hurt me." And I said, "I'm glad I asked because I want us to be able to work together. And for that to happen you can't abuse me, fight me, or stand against me because you are ticked off with another pastor."

Some people lost their passion because a pastor hurt them. Some pastor disappointed them. Some pastor broke their hearts. You should always respect your pastor—your spiritual leader. The Bible says in 1 Timothy 5:17-19,

> Let the elders who rule well be considered worthy of double honour, especially those who labour in preaching and teaching; for the scripture says, 'You shall not muzzle an ox while it is treading out the

grain', and, 'The labourer deserves to be paid.' Never accept any accusation against an elder except on the evidence of two or three witnesses.

You should always respect your pastor—and he or she should do the same for you. Honor your pastor. Respect your pastors; that doesn't mean you make them into gods. Pastors, spiritual leaders, are human beings; they are not gods. Therefore, they can flop; they are capable of failure. They can disappoint people. Just as you can fall short, pastors can fall short of what you expect. So honor your spiritual leaders but do not make them into gods.

DIVISIONS

Some people lost their passion because they were turned off by division in the church. In 1 Corinthians 1:10 Paul said, "Now I appeal to you, brothers and sisters, by the name of our Lord Jesus Christ, that all of you should be in agreement and that there should be no divisions among you, but that you should be united in the same mind and the same purpose."

To agree with one another, to not allow division, doesn't mean we won't have different views. You will have different views, but that doesn't mean you have to be divisive. Not being divisive means you deal with one another, speak and act in a way that will reduce arguments and increase harmony.

Some people don't understand this, and they allow their differences and the way they handle those differences to keep arguments going. They will fight others to the bitter end over pettiness. They will fight to the bitter end to have their way about a mission project or the color of the choir robes or where the water fountain should go, even if it means dividing the church. The pettiness, the differences in the church, will turn some people off.

In Psalm 42 we find a person who has lost his passion. He was in exile far from Jerusalem, mourning because he could no longer lead others in worshipping God in the temple. He was in a foreign land surrounded by foreign gods. He felt cut off from the Lord's presence. So his God passion—his fire for the Lord—was dimming. But this is not how God wanted him to be.

Regardless of what happens to you, God never wants you to lose your passion for Him. He never wants you to allow the world's trials and tribulations to put out your fire, your enthusiasm, your zeal. However, although God doesn't want you to allow this to happen, it can.

Some of us have let some moment, some event, some situation blow out our passion, and we need to reignite it. We need to have it lighted once more, set afire once more. If your passion for God has been blown out, how do you reignite it so that you can live a successful life today? Psalm 42 will help you answer this question.

BUILD UP AND NOT TEAR DOWN

Psalm 42:5 says, "Why are you cast down, O my soul…?" This was a tough time for the psalmist. He was a Korahite, a Levite family group who served as musicians from the time of David until the exile.

The psalmist is discouraged because he is exiled to a place far from Jerusalem and cannot worship in the temple or lead others in worshipping God. And so he gets into the "woe is me" state, tearing himself down.

But if you keep reading Psalm 42, you see that he eventually breaks free from this mindset. In verse 5b (the second half of the sentence) and part of 6, he says, "Hope in God; for I shall again praise him, my help and my God."

In this verse we see that the psalmist stops the "woe is me" mindset, tearing himself down, and starts to pick himself up. To reignite your passion for God, when tough times come learn to build yourself up and not tear yourself down. When tough times come, it will already be rough. You don't need to add to it. You don't need to make matters worse by saying depressing things to yourself. When tough times come (and they will) what you need is hope—you need to build yourself up and not tear yourself down.

Learn to forgive yourself. Don't let the tough times get you into a state of "if only I had done this...if only I had done that..." Whatever you did, you have to ask for forgiveness, forgive yourself, and move on with your life.

Yes, I understand that some of the trouble, some of the "woe is me" in your life, you put there yourself. Nobody did it to you but you: something stupid you did, the trouble you have, nobody did it but you—and I understand that. But what are you going to do, wallow in it? Keep putting yourself down? That's not going to solve anything.

But I will tell you what will help solve your lost passion problem and your "woe is me": forgiveness. Ask God for forgiveness, forgive yourself, and then move on with your life. The way you reignite your passion for God is not to tear yourself down but to build yourself up.

Don't keep tearing yourself down because you messed up. Okay, you fell short. So now ask for forgiveness—from God and yourself—so that you can get up, take advantage of another opportunity, another chance, another break that God is giving you.

Psalm 42:3 says, "My tears have been my food day and night while people say to me continually 'Where is your God?'" Verse 9 says, "God, my rock, 'Why have you forgotten me? Why must I walk about mournfully because the enemy oppresses me?'"

When I was in seminary, during chapel service I heard a preacher preach a sermon that I never forgot. He began his sermon with a statement, and after each statement he would ask the same question. The sermon went something like this: A plane crashed yesterday and all the people were killed...is it God's fault? A baby died this morning...is it God's fault? People are starving in Somalia...is it God's fault?

The preacher did this throughout his whole sermon. As he continued to say "Is it God's fault," I said to myself, *Are you out of your mind? These things are not God's fault.* I thought he was going to answer the question but he never did. He ended his sermon with "You decide."

So many times we blame God for all the world's troubles. The way you build yourself up and not tear yourself down is to not find fault with God. Many times when trouble shows up at our door, we blame God. He is not the problem. He is the answer.

Whenever you blame God for the world's evils, for your troubles, for your condition, you are traveling down the wrong road. Blame God? Stop! He is never your enemy. He is your friend. He is never your adversary. He is your supporter.

To reignite your passion for God, when tough times come, when adversity penetrates the lining in your life, learn to build yourself up and not tear yourself down. Seek forgiveness from God and yourself, and don't find fault with God. Hinder you, God doesn't. Help you, He does.

THE CHURCH IS IMPERFECT

Your passion for God can also be reignited by understanding that the church is not perfect. God is perfect but the church is not. Jimmy's English teacher was a perfectionist who demanded the very best of his pupils. So it was only to be expected that he would get furious when Little Jimmy handed in a poor paper.

"This is the worst essay it has ever been my misfortune to read," ranted the teacher. "It has too many mistakes. I can't understand how one person could make all these mistakes."

"One person didn't," replied Little Jimmy defensively. "My father helped me."

The church is made up of human beings, and human beings have flaws. Spots and blemishes, we have. We all make mistakes. Sometimes we make awful blunders. Sometimes these mistakes are unintentional because people are ignorant of what they are doing. This means that if someone hurt you maybe they were naïve, as we all are at times.

We try to do right, but because of original sin, the fall of Adam in the Garden of Eden, we have a propensity to mess up. Since we know the church is not perfect, what do we need to do?

When things are not done like you think they ought to be done, remember that sometimes, because human beings manage the church, it will fall short. Sometimes a "t" might not be crossed. Sometimes an "i" might not be dotted. But don't get all bent out of shape about it.

Have you ever heard of a church bulletin blooper? A church bulletin blooper is a mistake in the bulletin, a sentence or statement that doesn't say what the person meant to say. There was a church bulletin blooper going around a few years ago that said: "Don't let worry kill you…let the church help."

Do you let the petty mess in the church steal your joy? Don't let the petty mess in the church cause you to throw up your hands and quit coming to worship, quit coming to Bible study, quit coming to choir rehearsal. Don't let the petty mess cause you to abdicate your responsibilities.

Since you know the church is imperfect, not only should you not get all bent out of shape when things disappoint you, but don't stop doing your part to make things better. Part of being successful today is helping the church be successful.

So do your part to help the church move toward perfection, move towards excellence. The church can't do that if you don't do your part. The church can't do that if your ideology is to quit when things go wrong.

HELP OTHERS FIND CHRIST

The other way to reignite your passion is to do for others what was done for you. The Bible tells us about Jesus helping a man who was born blind. Jesus spit on the ground, made mud with the saliva, and spread the mud on the man's eyes, saying to him, "Go and wash in the pool of Siloam." When his neighbors saw him and saw that he was able to see, they asked, "How were your eyes opened?"

The blind man replied, "This man named Jesus spit onto the ground, made mud, and placed the mud on my eyes. He then told me to go and wash in the pool of Siloam, and I washed my eyes as I was told, and then I received my sight" (see John 9:25).

This blind man had a testimony, and like any of us who miraculously received our sight, I believe he repeatedly told his story. He told everyone he could about what Jesus had done for him. "Do you know

Reigniting Your Passion For God, Part 2

I was blind but now I see? Jesus did that for me. Come and let Him do it for you."

To reignite your passion for God, do for others what someone did for you: helped you to find Christ. You didn't come to Christ on your own. Someone—mother, father, brother, sister, friend, stranger—helped you to find the Lord. If they had not, your life would have been calamitous. If they had not, you would have never gotten that junk out of your trunk.

Recently, Mr. Goss and Mr. McCullough have been talking about the Walk to Emmaus, a spiritual renewal program that offers today's disciples an opportunity to rediscover Christ's presence in their lives. They talked about it so much that Mr. Nobles did the walk. Now Mr. Nobles is talking about it, and Mr. Chambers wants to do the walk.

To reignite your passion for God, do for others what someone did for you: helped you to get closer to Jesus. They helped your faith to germinate. Although you didn't want to hear about Jesus at the time, they didn't give up on you because they knew what Jesus could do. And one day you did hear, you did decide to let Jesus in, and now your song is "I was blind but now I see." And so you ought to be excited about helping others get closer to Jesus because someone helped you.

But this is not the only reason you should be excited. You should be excited about helping others find Jesus or get closer to Him because He is the doorway to deliverance. In Matthew 7:7 Jesus says, "Ask, and it will be given you; search and you will find; knock, and the door will be opened for you."

Whatever problems you are dealing with, Jesus is the doorway out of it. Whatever predicament you are in, Jesus is the doorway out of it. In Matthew 11:28, Jesus said, "Come to me, all you that are weary and carrying a heavy load, and I will give you rest." If you have really met Jesus, you ought to be filled with a desire to help others find the doorway. Why?

- Someone helped you to find it
- Someone helped you to discover it
- Someone helped you to open it
- Someone helped you to get through it

Without those people, you would still be vexed and trapped in your prison, trapped in your cage, trapped in your pigpen. Jesus is the doorway to deliverance. And those of us who have gone through that doorway know what it feels like after we did it.

You should be excited to help others find Jesus not only because He is the doorway to deliverance but also because His love never changes. First Peter 5:7 says, "Cast all your anxiety on him because he cares for you." Psalm 36:6 says, "Your steadfast love, O Lord, extends to the heavens, your faithfulness to the clouds." St. Augustine said, "God loves each of us as if there was only one of us."

People can be wishy-washy. They will love you today and hate you tomorrow. They can be your friend today, and your worst enemy tomorrow. But Jesus' love for you is never like this. His love for you never subsides. As someone said His love for you is deeper than the ocean and wider than the universe. He loved you before you first loved Him.

I heard someone summarize it well in a poem that went like this:

You ask me why I follow this Jesus.
Why I love him the way I do?
When the world turned away from his teachings
And the people who serve him are few
It's not the rewards I am after
Or gifts I hope to receive
It's the Presence that calls for commitment
It's the Spirit I trusted and believe…
I never know what comes tomorrow,
But I know I am never alone… (turnbacktogod.com/poem)

You reignite your passion for God by doing for others what people did for you: helped you to find Jesus. They helped you to find the Savior. They helped you to find your Knight in Shining Armor. And it wasn't a normal man. It wasn't a woman. It was Jesus, the King of Kings and Lord of Lords, the "on-time deliverer."

In Psalm 42:5-6, the psalmist says,

> Why are you cast down, O my soul,
>   and why are you disquieted within me?
> Hope in God; for I shall again praise him,
>   my help and my God.
> My soul is cast down within me;
>   therefore I remember you
> from the land of Jordan and of Hermon,
>   from Mount Mizar.

In Psalm 42:8, the psalmist says, "By day the LORD commands his steadfast love, and at night his song is with me, a prayer to the God of my life." Paraphrased, he was saying in the above verses, "Lord, when my soul is in the dumps, I rehearse everything I know of You; I think about all my blessings—all the ways You have been good to me. From the Jordan depths to the Hermon Heights, including Mount Mizar."

If I had written the same verses in this day and time, I would have said, "Lord, when I am down and out, I rehearse everything I know of You; I think about all my blessings—all the ways You have been good to me. Although my enemies have tried to vilify me, You have been good. From Greensboro, North Carolina, to Atlanta, Georgia, including when I was in South Africa."

God has been a blessing to all of us. You could not have come this far without God. Don't forget that. The last time you were hurting and were healed, the last time you were broken and put back together again, never could have happened without God. Don't forget that. It may be difficult right now, but God is going to give you the strength to make it, to take another step, to feel hope in your soul again.

A young man was getting ready to graduate from college. For many months he had admired a beautiful sports car in a dealer's showroom, and knowing that his father could well afford it, he told him that was all he wanted.

As graduation day approached, the young man awaited signs

that his father had purchased the car. Finally, on the morning of his graduation, his father called him into his private study. His father told him how proud he was to have such a fine son, and how much he loved him. He handed his son a beautifully wrapped gift box.

Curious, but somewhat disappointed, the young man opened the box and found a lovely leather-bound Bible with his name embossed in gold. He raised his voice to his father and said, "With all your money you give me a Bible?" and stormed out of the house, leaving the Bible.

Many years passed and the young man was very successful in business. He had a beautiful home and wonderful family. He realized his father was very old by now and thought perhaps he should go to see him.

He had not seen him since that graduation day. But before he could make arrangements, he received a telegram telling him his father had passed away and willed all of his possessions to him. He needed to come home immediately and take care of things.

When he arrived at his father's house, sadness and regret filled his heart. He began to search through his father's important papers and saw the still new Bible, just as he had left it years ago. With tears, he opened the Bible and turned the pages.

His father had carefully underlined a verse, Matthew 7:11: "And if ye, being evil, know how to give good gifts to your children, how much more shall your Father which is in heaven, give to those who ask him?"

Living A Successful Life Today

As he read those words, a car key dropped from the back of the Bible. It had a tag with the dealer's name, the same dealer that owned the sports car he had desired. On the tag was the date of his graduation and the words PAID IN FULL.

How many times have we missed God's blessings because they were not packaged as we expected? So many times we lose our passion for God because we think He has not blessed us. We think we have not received what we deserve. But every day you get up you have to remember that God has not forgotten you. You have to remember that He is always blessing you; you just have to take the time to look.

Despite the cumbersome hardships you may have experienced, despite the tormenting troubles you may have encountered, despite the difficult duties you may have to perform, you are still blessed.

You can reignite your passion for God by recognizing your blessings, taking the time to look, taking the time to thank Him. It might not always be what you want, but it will be what you need. It might not always come when you want, but it will come when you most need it. To reignite your passion for God, count your blessings. Take the time to look because His blessings for you are all around you. His miracles for you are all around you. His goodness for you is all around you. His grace for you is all around you.

Count your blessings. Take the time to look. You got up this morning—that's a blessing. He watched over you last night—that's a blessing. It's no secret what God can do because what He's done for others, He can do for you—that's a blessing. Every breath of air is a blessing; every beat of our hearts is a blessing; every bite of food is a blessing; every night of rest is a blessing.

CHAPTER FIVE

Managing Stress, Part 1

READ THE SCRIPTURE: Genesis 35:1-8

God said to Jacob, 'Arise, go up to Bethel, and settle there. Make an altar there to the God who appeared to you when you fled from your brother Esau.' So Jacob said to his household and to all who were with him, 'Put away the foreign gods that are among you, and purify yourselves, and change your clothes; then come, let us go up to Bethel, that I may make an altar there to the God who answered me in the day of my distress and has been with me wherever I have gone.' So they gave to Jacob all the foreign gods that they had, and the rings that were in their ears; and Jacob hid them under the oak that was near Shechem.

As they journeyed, a terror from God fell upon the cities all around them, so that no one pursued them. Jacob came to Luz (that is, Bethel), which is in the land of Canaan, he and all the people who were with him, and there he built an altar and called the place El-bethel,* because it was there that God had revealed himself to him when he fled from his brother. And Deborah, Rebekah's nurse, died, and she was buried under an oak below Bethel. So it was called Allon-bacuth.

Managing Stress, Part 1

Are you under stress? Are you being pestered by one problem after another? Every one of us at one time or another has had to deal with stress. In this world, stress abounds. Jesus said in the world you are going to have trouble. He could have said it this way: in the world you are going to have stress.

A father stayed home one night to watch his son while his wife went to a PTA meeting. Later in the evening he settled down to watch TV. But his son repeatedly kept coming in and asking for a glass of water.

After the fifth glass, the dad lost his patience and yelled, "I'm trying to watch TV. Go to bed!"

"But Dad," the boy whined, "my room is still on fire!"

Every person, young or old, black or white, Protestant or Catholic, has had to deal with stress. Stress is going up and down streets and in and out of homes seeking whomever it can detour. If you are not careful, protracted stress can get inside your body and eat you from the inside out. This very moment stress is eating some of us alive.

Stress consumes us because we don't take advice well. Do you take advice well? Are you able to receive counsel from your pastor, friend, mother, or father?

A man walks up to a cashier in a grocery store and says, "Hey, how much for these jalapeño peppers?" He pronounces it "joe-la-pen-oh," not "ho-lo-peen-yo."

The cashier says, "Sir, that's not what those peppers are called."

The man replies, "Listen, buddy, this is America, and I can

pronounce any word the way I please."

The cashier responds, "That may be, sir, but those are green peppers."

Stress is eating some of us alive because when people try to advise us, we don't listen. We are going to do whatever we want to do, whenever we want to do it, however we want to do it, even if it is wrong. This attitude foreshadows your doom.

Could it be that your unsuccessful living stems from you not listening? People give you advice but you just won't listen. Your friends try to admonish you by giving you a caveat, telling you that you are getting ready to step into a six-foot ditch. But, oh no, you think people are making much ado about nothing. You know what you are doing, and you don't need anyone to telling you anything. If we were rubber bands, people could see the stress marks, the weak spots in us that are about to pop.

Yet we won't take any advice, advice that will keep us from being pulverized by stress, advice that will help us, heal us, and hold us together so that we don't fall apart. Are you able to receive advice? Or do you have tomorrow's paper in your back pocket?

In Genesis 35:1, God said to Jacob, "Arise, go up to Bethel, and settle there. Make an altar there to the God who appeared to you when you fled from your brother Esau." Jacob is in the midst of trying and hectic times. He recently left his job with his father-in-law. He was reconciled with his brother after twenty years. His daughter was raped. His sons have just massacred an entire town making his family unwelcome everywhere.

In this story about Jacob, you see stress licking his fingers and lips because stress is eating Jacob alive. With all this going on in Jacob's life, he feels stress consuming him. He feels stress biting away at him. But also in our text, we see Jacob trying to manage his stress. He doesn't seek to let his stress manage him, but he seeks to manage his stress.

God wants you to manage your stress, not let it manage you. He wants you to maintain control when situations, systems, and society make excessive demands on you. Don't allow them to send you adrift.

When stress grabs you by the collar and demands you to move in a certain direction, demands you to listen, or demands you to act now, reach up and take the hands of stress off your collar, look stress straight in the eyes, and say, "You wait a minute, and let me tell you something—I'm in charge. You are not going to make me do something I don't want to do, something I am not ready to do, or something that is not in my best interest or the interest of those I love."

Letting stress manage you is not what God wants; He wants you to manage it. The question is how do you do that? The answers are in Genesis 35:1-3.

SOMETHING YOU NEED TO CHANGE

In Genesis 35:2, the Bible says, "So Jacob said to his household and to all who were with him, 'Put away the foreign gods that are among you, and purify yourselves, and change your clothes....'"

Living A Successful Life Today

In some translations, that word "foreign gods" is "idols." Some of the Israelites had "idols," or foreign gods, in their houses, even though they worshipped the one true God you and I worship. What is an idol? An idol is anything—a thought, a physical object, a good luck charm, a desire—we put before God. Jacob ordered his household to get rid of their idols, their foreign gods.

The idols need to be removed because they can ruin your life and rot your faith. They can keep you from maturing spiritually, keep you on the wrong path, and lead you to the city called destruction. Think about it. Are there any idols in your life that you need to remove?

You can remove those idols by taking a look at your life and seeing if there is something you can change or something you can give up. All of us have something in our lives that we need to change or give up: a bad habit, a bad behavior, a bad desire, a bad activity... No one is perfect, perfect in our talk, perfect in our Christian walk, perfect in our faith. No one is without spot or blemish.

The habits and customs of the Eskimos of North Alaska have remained very much the same for five hundred years until recently. They had to depend on catching the polar bear for meat, for clothing (the bear's fur), for fat for cooking, and for tools (the bear's bones and teeth).

However, you don't just go out and catch a polar bear. The polar bear is too big for a man to take head-on, so the Eskimos developed an ingenious way of catching them. First of all, the Eskimos kill a small seal and drag the carcass across the snow leaving a trail of blood.

They then take a double-edged knife and freeze the long handle about two feet deep into the snow, leaving the double-edged blade sticking out. Afterward, they place the carcass over the blade and then wait patiently.

The polar bear finds the tracks of blood in the snow, follows the tracks, and finds an easy meal. Once he bows his head, folds his hands, and says his grace, he starts to eat. Soon the delicacy is gulped down.

The Eskimos are smart; they know that if they take a small seal rather than a large seal, the bear will still be incredibly hungry even after eating the seal. He devours the little seal and licks the blade, trying to see if there are any small pieces of the seal left. Just as some of us used to lick the bowl when our mothers or grandmothers made a pie, the bear licks and licks and licks.

Now remember the bear is drawn to his food by the taste of blood. The more he licks the more he tastes blood—his own blood. In fact, it is the taste of his own blood that kills him. The blood is the fatal attraction for the bear.

Your bad habits, desires, or callous behaviors, those things you have a propensity to keep doing, can destroy you as you keep licking and licking and licking them. They can bring stress into your life that wrecks your relationships, your health, and your outlook on life.

When you have habits in your life that you know are not good for you, you do yourself and your loved ones a disservice because these habits—things you need to change, things that make you unkind and mean and selfish—will eventually drown you and may also take under those whom you love.

Bad habits, things you need to let go, can incapacitate you, keep you in a quagmire, suck out your joy, and choke your destiny. So if you want to manage stress in your life, ask yourself:

- Do I need to change this?
- Do I need to give this up?
- Do I need to let go of this?
- Do I need to stop doing this?
- Do I need to get rid of some idols?

After you take a good look at your life and decide what you need to change, what you need to let go, decide that you are *going to change it*.

Genesis 35:1-2 says, "God said to Jacob, 'Arise, go up to Bethel, and settle there. Make an altar there to the God who appeared to you when you fled from your brother Esau.' So Jacob said to his household and to all who were with him, 'Put away the foreign gods that are among you, and purify yourselves, and change your clothes....'"

When Jacob receives this message from God, he has a lot of stress in his life; when God shows Jacob what to do to manage this stress, which is to go to Bethel and build an altar, Jacob decides to

Managing Stress, Part 1

do what God said. He decides that a change is needed. He decides that he needs to clean up some things in his household, so he tells all those in his household to get rid of the idols.

After you look around and decide what you need to change, take the necessary steps to change. Do you want your life replenished and restored? Then take the necessary steps. Some people see what they need to change, but that is all they do—see. They don't seek to change; they just talk about change, plan to change, list things to change. But they never take any actions after that.

Why? Because some of us believe it is easier to fix the blame than to fix the problem. But fixing the blame keeps the stress in your life because you never deal with the true cause of the stress. Let me ask you again: do you want to manage the stress in your life? Do you want to grip the handle of your stress and not let it grip the handle of your life, turning you up and down, and around and around?

After you find the thing in your life that you need to change, after you find the idol in your life that you need to let go of, decide you are going to change it; decide that you are going to let it go. Don't keep allowing those things to put winkles in your face faster than winkles are supposed to be there. That's asinine. Don't keep allegiance to the idols in your life that are causing you to wring your hands and pace the floor all night, every night.

After you decide to change, set yourself small, easy goals. Refrain from doing too much too soon. For example, if stress is causing you to eat the whole chocolate cake and a pint of milk, set a goal to eat half the chocolate cake and one glass of milk. Set small, easy goals.

Then set the date that you are going to begin putting the changes in place. It does no good to say you are going to change something in your life or let go of something, but you procrastinate or never get started. One of the reasons why some of us never get started is because we never set a start date. We never post a date on our calendar. We say,

- "Someday I'm going to stop procrastinating."
- "Someday I'm going to tithe."
- "Someday I'm going to stop eating that particular food I know is not good for me."

Let me say something that you might not know. "Someday" is not a date. "Someday" is not included on the calendar. To manage the stress in your life, look around and see what you need to change; decide to change; set small, easy goals; then set a date that you are going to change or get rid of that idol, that thing or place or person you are putting before God.

When Jacob told the people to get rid of their idols—and their earrings, which were their good luck charms used to ward off evil—he was asking a whole lot. Telling the Israelites to get rid of their idols was like telling them to throw away what could be the winning lottery ticket.

Managing Stress, Part 1

What's the Holy Spirit saying to you about managing stress in this part of the story? The Holy Spirit is saying "Be willing to make a sacrifice." Yes, doing all the things I just mentioned will require a sacrifice.

There are some things for which you need to say to yourself "I'm stopping this. And I am stopping this now." There are some goals, such as tithing, attending Bible study, and Sunday school, for which you need to say to yourself "I'm going to start doing this now. I'm not waiting until tomorrow. I'm going to do this now. I'm not waiting until I think I can do it. I'm going to do what God says and step out in faith and do this now, not tomorrow, not the next day or next week or next year, but now!"

There are some things you need to do now. The longer you wait the longer you will be without everything God said He would do for you. The longer you put it off the longer you are going to be weighed down with stress you can't manage. So today do what needs to be done. Get rid of your idols now. Tomorrow may be too late. Stress will take you out—defeat you—if you don't. Is this all you can do to manage stress? No, there is something else.

TECHNIQUES TO RELEASE STRESS

One lady said, "I have changed my system for labeling homemade freezer meals. I used to carefully note in large clear letters, 'Meatloaf' or 'Pot Roast' or 'Steak and Vegetables' or 'Chicken and Dumplings' or 'Beef Pot Pie.' However, I used to get very frustrated when I asked my husband what he wanted for dinner because

Living A Successful Life Today

he never asked for any of those things. So I decided to stock the freezer with what he really likes.

"If you look in my freezer now you'll see a whole new set of labels. You'll find dinners with neat, legible tags that say 'Whatever,' 'Anything,' 'I Don't Know,' 'I Don't Care,' 'Something Good,' or 'Food.' My frustration is reduced because no matter what my husband replies when I ask him what he wants for dinner, I know that it will be there waiting."

You can manage your stress by finding techniques you can use that work for you, that release stress. There are some techniques you can practice that will adjust the heat. When you are dealing with stress, that's heat. When you are dealing with financial problems, marital problems, children problems, these things are full of heat.

It may be hot in the kitchen of your life, but there are some things that work for you—it may not work for anybody else, but it will work for you—to cool off your kitchen, bring down the heat.

I read about some people who have weird stress techniques that work just for them. One man, when he is stressed out, goes outside and feels the grass for sixty seconds. Another man said he goes outside and climbs a tree barefoot. He said this can hurt if you don't pick the right tree. So he recommends choosing a tree with smooth bark.

Someone else said that when they are stressed out they walk around their office backward. To manage stress, find some

Managing Stress, Part 1

techniques you can use to cool off the heat of the stress. Let me give you some specific techniques you can do to manage stress.

Genesis 35:1 says, "God said to Jacob, 'Arise, go up to Bethel, and settle there. Make an altar there to the God who appeared to you when you fled from your brother Esau.'" The place where Jacob was having all the problems—where he lost his job, where his daughter was raped, where his sons massacred a whole town—notice God told him to leave that place.

One technique you can use to manage stress is to remove yourself from the stressful situation. Sometimes all you need to do is get away from the thing or person or place that has you full of steam.

This is necessary for all of us—to get away from the thing or person or place that has us full of steam because we are like steam pots. Once we get full of steam we pop our lid.

That's why sometimes simple things can make you pop your lid, causing you to go off, causing you to be touchy, causing you to be insensitive because you are already full of steam. Sometimes you need to find a place where you can go to let off some steam and simmer down:

- A room in your house
- The library
- The school track
- A walk in the neighborhood
- A drive on the interstate

- A vacation
- A good book to read

Any of these places could be a place of release for you. But you have to decide.

My grandmother raised me. I remember times when stress had engulfed her. I could see it in her face. Whenever she got this way, I remember hearing her in the kitchen singing or humming. She would sing or hum "I don't feel no ways tired. I don't believe he brought me this far to leave me."

Or she would sing or hum "My hope is built on nothing less than Jesus' blood and righteousness. I dare not trust the sweet frame but wholly lean on Jesus' name. On Christ the solid rock I stand. All other ground is sinking sand. All other ground is sinking sand."

When you are about to pop your lid, sing or hum a song you know, not a sad song. Some people get stressed out and they sing sad songs like

> I gave you my Cadillac keys, you don't drive
> I hired you a limousine, you won't ride
> Bought you the house on the hill, you hate the view
> Even wrote you into my will, gave you something to look forward to
>
> But girl, you know, what hurts me the most
> Is I gave all my love to you
> All you ever give me
> All you ever give me

All you ever give me is the blues
Nothing but the blues (B.B. King)

When you are about to pop your lid, sing something inspiring, something like

Jesus is all the world to me,
My life, my joy, my all;
He is my strength from day to day, Without Him I would fall.
When I am sad, to Him I go,
No other one can cheer me so;
When I am sad, He makes me glad,
He's my Friend.

God spoke to Jacob: "Go back to Bethel. Stay there and build an altar to the God who revealed himself to you when you were running for your life from your brother Esau." Jacob told his family and all those who lived with him, "Throw out all the alien gods which you have, take a good bath, and put on clean clothes, we're going to Bethel. I'm going to build an altar there to the God who answered me when I was in trouble and who has stuck with me everywhere I've gone since."

You can manage stress not only by using techniques that help you release stress but also by not focusing on the problems. Don't focus on the pressures. Don't focus on the things that have you stressed out, that make you feel like you are standing under a tree loaded with birds doing their business on you.

But focus on God who crafted the universe, God who taught

the mockingbird how to sing, God who dug out the earth with His hands, took His cup and poured water in holes and called them rivers, streams, seas, and oceans.

Focus on God. That's where your mind should be. That's where your heart should be. There's where your soul should be. Focus on God, not your paradox. Why? Focusing on God will draw you closer to Him. It will bring you nearer to Him. Focusing on God will give you the strength you need to manage the stress in your life that you thought you never could control.

You see, Jacob knew if he was going to deal with all the stress in his life, he needed God. He knew God was his panacea. There are some things you can't handle alone because some things need divine intervention; some things are bigger than the muscles you have, and some things are cleverer than your intelligence.

Not too long ago we had storms that knocked out our lights. When the lights went out, I lit the candles in the house and got the flashlight. However, when I cut on the flashlight, it wouldn't work. Why? Because the battery had drained. In fact, it had corroded inside the flashlight.

The sun is not like a battery. The sun is constant and reliable. It is so reliable and constant that few of us rarely acknowledge its existence. According to scientists, the sun is one of the primary reasons that life exists on earth. It has hidden benefits that prove it is a lot more than a gigantic lamp that lights our daily activities. It is a living, breathing organism.

Managing Stress, Part 1

Moments come in this life that require more strength than you are able to produce. You see our strength is like a battery. It eventually drains. It eventually corrodes. Conversely, God's strength is like the sun. All you have to do is sit under it awhile and you are energized, given more strength and other benefits too numerous to count.

When stress grabs ahold of you, turn your head and look toward God because that is where your strength will come from to break you loose.

- Worrying about the situation won't help you to handle it.
- Crying over the stress in your life won't get rid of the stress.
- Putting on a front for everyone, pretending like everything is all right, just makes matters worse because you never take steps to deal with it.

You might not want anyone to know what you are dealing with. You may be too embarrassed. But never be too private to tell God. Never be too embarrassed to tell God all about your troubles. He knows already anyway.

- God is the only One who can give you the strength you need to manage your stress.
- God is the only One who can keep you from snapping like a rubber band.
- God is the only One who can keep you from being stretched

too far because He knows just how much you can bear. He knows when you are at a dead end.

Turn to God and He will show you a path through your weeds and brushes of stress. Turn to God and pray, "Lord, show me the way." And He will show you. Turn to God and pray, "Lord, I don't know what to do. I don't know how to handle this. I'm going under from the weight of my stress. Show me what to do."

And the Lord will make your rough places smooth, your crooked places straight, and your burdens bearable. That's the switch that will work for you. That's the switch that will turn down the heat of your stress. That's the switch that will turn the light on so you can see your way clear. Focus on God.

CHAPTER SIX

Managing Stress, Part 2

READ THE SCRIPTURE: Numbers 11:1-6

Now when the people complained in the hearing of the LORD about their misfortunes, the LORD heard it and his anger was kindled. Then the fire of the LORD burned against them, and consumed some outlying parts of the camp. But the people cried out to Moses; and Moses prayed to the LORD, and the fire abated. So that place was called Taberah, because the fire of the LORD burned against them.

The rabble among them had a strong craving; and the Israelites also wept again, and said, 'If only we had meat to eat! We remember the fish we used to eat in Egypt for nothing, the cucumbers, the melons, the leeks, the onions, and the garlic; but now our strength is dried up, and there is nothing at all but this manna to look at.'

Someone said, "With computers doing our thinking, all we need now is a worrying machine." Someone else said, "An educated man will sit up all night and worry over things a fool never

Living A Successful Life Today

dreamed of." Then I overheard someone say in the store the other day, "Why worry about the future? With all the bombs, politicians, and pollution, there may not be one."

In the last chapter I talked about stress, how it affects us, and what we need to do about it. Stress! when you take on more than you can handle. Stress! when you are rushing around because you put too much on your calendar. Stress! when you think about tomorrow's problems, when you don't know if you are even going to see tomorrow. I want to continue highlighting this ailment called stress because this subject is important to living a successful life today.

GET THE BEST OF YOU

In 1994, *U.S. News and World Report* reported a story about a man name Kevin Carter. The article said Kevin Carter could never escape his continent's turmoil. For a decade the photographer captured vivid pictures of repression and strife in his native South Africa.

One year he went to famine-wracked Sudan and came upon a starving toddler stalked by a vulture. He photographed the scene—an image that won him the Pulitzer Prize—then chased the vulture away. As the child resumed her walk to a feeding station, he lit a cigarette and wept. At age thirty-three, he killed himself with carbon monoxide pumped into his pickup truck. Explained his father: "Kevin always carried around the horror of the work he did." (*U.S. News and World Report*, August 8, 1994)

First, managing stress is important because if you don't learn how to manage it, it will eventually get the best of you. Stress can bruise you both inside and out if it goes unchecked.

Stress is having a field day with some of us. It is running all over us. It is turning flips and twists in every corner of our lives. It has built a sandbox in some of our homes, and it's playing with our minds, playing with our health, playing with our relationship with God.

One mother said, "I always talked about my job a lot at home, and my young daughter had always expressed great interest. So I thought it would be a treat for her to spend the day with me at the office. Since I wanted it to be a surprise, I didn't tell her where we were going, just that it would be fun. Although usually a bit shy, she seemed excited to meet each colleague I introduced. On the way home, however, she seemed somewhat down.

"'Didn't you have a nice time?' I asked."

"'Well, it was okay,' she responded. 'But I thought it would be more like a circus.'

Confused, I asked, 'Whatever do you mean?' She said, 'Well, you said you work with a bunch of clowns, and I never got to see them!'"

Second, managing stress is important because stress can make you say and do things you never meant to say and do. It can make you act out of character. It can make you do dastardly deeds when you are really a nice person. Although you may be pleasant, stress can strip you of that and make you come across as angry, miserable,

Living A Successful Life Today

and messy. You don't want that—do you?

In Numbers 11:1 we find these words: "Now when the people complained in the hearing of the LORD about their misfortunes, the LORD heard it and his anger was kindled. Then the fire of the LORD burned against them, and consumed some outlying parts of the camp."

In this text, we see Moses and the Israelites under the foot of stress. The Israelites feel that God has abandoned them, and Moses is tired of hearing them complain. The Israelites have now been in the wilderness for awhile.

The book of Leviticus covers only one month of the forty-year journey to the Promised Land. But the book of Numbers records thirty-nine years of wandering in the desert. Chapter 11 is still in the first year of the journey, but the people are tired and road-weary. And, as you will see, their leader, Moses, is a little weary too. The Israelites feel under the feet of stress and so does Moses.

But the Israelites' journey in the wilderness was not meant for them to allow stress to kick them around. It was not meant to beat them down, bruise their spirits, and put a hole in their faith. Furious with them for complaining and allowing stress to wrestle them to the ground, God set the outer boundaries of the camp on fire.

God gets upset with us when we allow this old gray-haired world to defeat us. He didn't claw up dirt, mold us, make us, and set us on this planet to allow stress to have its way with us. When God first thought of making us, His intent was always for us to manage

Managing Stress, Part 2

our situations and not our situations—stress, worry, depression, and fear—to manage us.

God created a perfect world. But we messed it up. How? The same way we are messing it up now: disobedience, rebellion, defiance, non-compliance. He says go left. We go right. He says sit still. We get up and move. It would be helpful if you keep in mind that whatever He tells you to do, it's always for your good.

Although He created you and gave you free will to choose what kind of relationship you are going to have with Him, God always hopes that you are going to choose His way. None of us is perfect, as you have heard me say throughout this book. So one day something may happen in your life, and you may not make the right choice—and end up under stress.

But even when this happens, even when you make wrong choices, even when you take the wrong road and your soul's engine gets in mechanical trouble on that road, God put some tools in place, some service stations along the way to help you fix your trouble.

Why? Because He told us in Romans 8:28, "We know that in all things God works for the good of those who love him, who have been called according to his purpose." In other words, God doesn't want the stressors of this life to outscore us. He doesn't want us defeated. He doesn't want stress to cause us to throw in the towel.

He wants us to sit stress down and say to those stressors, "I'm in charge. A lot is coming my way. But I am in charge. And you are not going to cause me to release hormones in my body that raise my blood pressure, produce ulcers, produce diabetes, give me mood swings and bad relationships, speed up my heart and breathing, halt my digestion, cause a surge in my blood sugar, and more. Mr. Stressor, I'm in charge."

Manage your stress, manage your anxiety, manage the traffic of issues that drive your way—that is what God wants. He doesn't want stress managing you. Well, you say, how can I manage my stress?

TAKING CHARGE

You have to take charge. You have to roll up your sleeves and take control of the situations in your life. People who do not take charge of their lives, their spiritual and physical lives, become disrupted, forcing them into a rhythm of annoying singsong. In other words, people who do not take charge of their lives allow anything and everything to happen to them—it is not a pretty sight: depression, alcoholism, drug addiction, homelessness, bankruptcy. Take charge. Take control.

You need to take charge also because the wrong thoughts can lead you to the wrong actions that can get you in trouble.

I read a story about a man whose wrong thoughts led him to the wrong action. He said,

"When our lawnmower broke and wouldn't run, my wife kept hinting to me that I should get it fixed. But somehow I always had something else to take care of first: the truck, the car, fishing, always something more important to me. Finally she thought of a clever way to make her point.

"When I arrived home one day, I found her seated in the tall grass, busily snipping away with a tiny pair of sewing scissors. I watched silently for a short time and then went into the house. I was gone only a few minutes. When I came out again I handed her a toothbrush.

"'When you finish cutting the grass,' I said, 'you might as well sweep the sidewalk.'

The doctors say I will walk again, but I will always have a limp."

Take charge. Take control because the wrong thoughts can lead you to the wrong actions that can get you in trouble. Take charge of what?

Take charge of your thoughts. Numbers 11:4-6 says,

> The rabble among them had a strong craving; and the Israelites also wept again, and said, 'If only we had meat to eat! We remember the fish we used to eat in Egypt for nothing, the cucumbers, the melons, the leeks, the onions, and the garlic; but now our strength is dried up, and there is nothing at all but this manna to look at.'

When the Israelites didn't have the kind of food they wanted they became austere towards God and filled with fear. Fear grabbed hold of their thoughts. With those fears came stress, and the result was this:

- They forget that God had their back.
- They forgot that God brought them out of slavery.
- They forgot that God didn't bring them out of slavery to let them starve in the wilderness.

And so they complained about how good they had it when they were in slavery in Egypt. They let fear control their thoughts. You manage stress by controlling your thinking. You can't let your thoughts run rampant up and down the paths of your life and create a fiasco. Unchecked, your thoughts will drag you down any path: paths of doubt, paths of abuse, paths of anger, paths of apathy, paths of temptation. Unchecked, your thoughts can deplete your strength instead of replenish it.

You have to get control of your thoughts if you want to manage stress because if you don't you will become unraveled at the seams. Thoughts will run toward you from everywhere. You have to control them if you want relief.

You can't let the crowd of thoughts running at you every day decide what the day is going to be like. For you see, God put you in charge of your mind, so you have to decide what you are going to let your mind think about. The story of Adam and Eve's rebellion against God illustrates what happens if you don't.

God said to Adam and Eve, "Don't eat from this tree. You can eat from any tree except the Tree of Knowledge of Good and Evil." But after God gave these instructions, the devil with his cold-eyed demeanor steps into the picture and says to Eve, "I know God told you not to eat from the tree in the middle of the garden because He said if you did you would die. That's not true."

As the devil continues to lead Eve down the path of destruction, he strokes his mustache like a villain and chuckles malevolently. "You won't die. God doesn't want you to eat from that tree because it will make you just like Him: knowing everything, ranging all the way from good to evil."

So what does Eve do? She begins to feel a paradox in what God said and what the devil said, which leads her to eat from the forbidden tree and convince her husband to do likewise. Adam and Eve couldn't go the distance with the command God had given them.

The devil made Eve feel God was imprecise. God is never imprecise when He talks to us. When God tells us something, He never leaves a gray area. He is always clear. But the devil made Eve feel otherwise. How did he do this? He sent the wrong thoughts to Adam and Eve's minds.

Notice God didn't stop the thought from entering them. He told them they had to stop the thought of eating from the forbidden tree from ever entering their minds. "Don't think about that tree" is what God said. Adam and Eve had a problem doing what God said do. Perhaps God would have helped them resist the temptation if they had asked. But they didn't.

God put you in charge of your mind, so you have to decide what you are going to let through the cracks. It is your decision. God is not going to decide for you. He will give you the choices you have and then the best choice, but He will not make the decision. Controlling your thoughts is imperative. It will help you decipher what God is saying about the choice you need to make. The salient question at this point is how can you control your thoughts?

Identify what is causing the stressful thoughts. What is causing you to be an unhappy camper? You may be stressed out, but you don't know what has you stressed out.

- Could it be growing pains?
- Could it be too much to do?
- Could it be moving to a new home or school?
- Could it be family problems?

After school one day, a first-grade boy was sitting at the kitchen table, eating his afternoon snack, when he blurted out, "Mom, the teacher was asking me today if I have any brothers or sisters who will be coming to school."

The boy's mother replied, "That's nice of her to take such an interest, dear. What did she say when you told her you are the only child?"

"She just said, 'Thank goodness!'"

Pinpoint what is producing the nerve-wracking feeling that you have. You may be stressed out, but you don't know why. Stress can't

Managing Stress, Part 2

be dealt with if you don't know what it is. Finding the thought that is causing the stress is your first challenge because you could think it is one thing but it is another.

For example, there are people who are on edge, and they think it's stress on their job that's making them feel that way, but it's really stress in their homes. There are people who think they are worried about an assignment, but they're really worried about a sick loved one.

What is causing the stressful thoughts? What is causing the anxiety to build up poisonous fumes in your life? What is causing you to make flippant remarks? That's what you need to find out. That's what you need to bring to the forefront so that you can see it and deal with it.

In Numbers 11:4 the Scripture says, "The rabble among them had a strong craving; and the Israelites also wept again, and said, 'If only we had meat to eat!'" No matter what God did for the Israelites they always managed to allow the wrong thoughts to step into their minds: rebellious thoughts, negative thoughts, mean thoughts, unruly thoughts. And these thoughts got them in trouble with God.

Once you have identified the stressful thoughts, make a conscious effort to stop the thoughts. Be aware of how these thoughts make you feel. Be aware of your behavior whenever certain thoughts start pulling your mind around, because when you become aware of how you feel, you will know when to take the ropes off your mind by saying to those thoughts, "You are not going to drag me around. You are not going to make me feel bad today. You are not going to haul me around and scar me anymore."

You control your thoughts by making a conscious effort to become aware of the times your thoughts are dragging you around. Your thinking, you have to take charge of. Negative views that come your way, you have to control. Nobody can do that for you. You have to do that for yourself. Does this statement have a familiar ring for you?

Another way to control your thoughts is to see them as images that are on the outside of you trying to enter. This is a powerful image because, with the help of God, once you can see the thoughts as images or figures outside yourself you can begin to manage them. You can begin to use your mind to push and thrust and drive negative thoughts away.

Paul said it this way in Philippians 4:8: "Whatever is true, whatever is noble, whatever is right, whatever is pure, whatever is lovely, whatever is admirable—if anything is excellent or praiseworthy—think about such things." Paul said use your mind to push away the damaging winds of negative thoughts. Your mind is powerful.

- It can help you or destroy you.
- It can enable you or disable you.
- It can make things possible or make things impossible.
- It can make things doable or make things undoable.

Managing Stress, Part 2

Your mind is powerful. So use it to buttress yourself, to push away negative thoughts that try to leap into your life and unravel it: unravel your destiny, unravel your relationship with the church, unravel your relationship with God. To manage stress, you have to take charge of your thoughts. To stop coming off as a loose screw, you have to control how thoughts affect you. You have to control what thoughts do to you because if you don't the hospital is waiting, Prozac is waiting, bad health is waiting.

Let's look at Numbers 11:4 again. It says, "The rabble among them had a strong craving; and the Israelites also wept again, and said, 'If only we had meat to eat!'" God had delivered the Israelites out of Pharaoh's evil hands, set them free, and watched over them as they traveled to the Promised Land, and all they could think about were fish, cucumbers, melons, leeks, onions, and garlic. However, the most important thing was that they were free. They were no longer under the whip of Pharaoh. But the Israelites couldn't see this.

In addition to controlling your thoughts by seeing thoughts as images that are on the outside of you trying to enter, you can also control your thoughts by deciding what is important. Life is full of choices, and if you are not sure what is important to you, life will have you running in all directions.

Whenever you permit your life to be pulled in all directions, your life begins to tear apart leaving little holes that become big holes that become gaping holes. That's when you start feeling empty, unfulfilled, unhappy, discontent, disgruntled, and disgusted.

And then you allow these feelings to begin to write your obituary.

J.I. Packer wrote,

> Satan wants to see every minute misused; it is for us to make every minute count for God. How? Not by a frenzied rushing to pack a quart of activity into a pint pot of time (a common present-day error), but by an ordered life-style in which, within the set rhythm of toil and rest, work and worship, due time is allotted to sleep, family, wage-earning, homemaking, prayer, recreation, and so on, so that we master time instead of being mastered by it. (J.I. Packer (1996, c1994) *Growing in Christ*. Originally published *I want to be a Christian*. Wheaton, Ill.: Tyndale House Publishers, c1977; Index (252), Wheaton, Ill.: Crossway Books)

Some of us are spread out over life like rubber bands wrapped around too many envelopes because we don't know what is important. Do you know what is important in your life? If so, what are those things?

The Lord had given the Israelites instructions, appeared to them, unlocked their prison cell, and set them free from Pharaoh. The children of Israel were on their way, and the first thing they did was complain. Then the Lord's anger burst into flames against them, and that blaze destroyed some of the people on the outskirts of the camp.

After hearing their complaints to Moses, it is as if God gave them something to complain about through the fire that broke out in their midst. Then the people screamed to Moses for help, and when he "looked to the heaven from whence cometh his help" and

Managing Stress, Part 2

prayed to the Lord, the fire stopped. After that the area was known as Taberah (which means "the place of burning"), because fire from the Lord had burned among them there.

The Israelites complained, and then Moses complained. But God responded positively to Moses and negatively to the rest of the people. Notice that when the people thought they could not keep their heads above water, when they thought God had abandoned them, they complained to one another and nothing was accomplished. Moses delivered his complaint to God, who could solve any problem.

To manage stress, don't hit the ceiling or explode with anger, but take your stress to God. Take your anxieties to God. You see, the heart of the matter is you get bent out of shape when you start thinking about what you don't have instead of looking at what you do have.

If you have given your life to Christ, confess with your mouth and believe in your heart that Jesus is Lord and you have what is important. God has been around before time, but He is not some gray-haired old man with a hearing aid in each ear. He is still vibrant, still amazing, still powerful, still a heavy hitter. When you have Him, you have what is important.

- Everything might not be going your way, but you still have God.
- Storm clouds might be hanging over your head, but you still

have God.
- Winds of opposition might be blowing in your life, but you still have God.

And as long as you have God, you can make it. As long as you have God, you are still in the game. Taking yourself out of the game of life is not what you need to do. You haven't fouled out. You haven't lost the game. You still have some more time left on your clock.

The stress is always going to be there trying to block you, pull you down, keep you from winning. But you don't have to worry. You don't have to let stress wear you out. When it gets too much, take whatever it is to God because He is on your team. He is ready to help you out. He is ready to give you relief. He is ready to break you out.

So if you want to manage your stress, then do all the things I have talked about, but don't forget you have a Superstar on your team. Don't forget you have a player on your team whose name is God, and because He is on your team everything is going to be all right, if you trust Him.

- You are going to make it if you trust Him.
- You are going to defeat your worries if you bring your worries to Him and trust Him.
- You are going to get through your dark moment if you trust Him.

Managing Stress, Part 2

I don't know what your stress is but God does. I don't know how much more you can bear but God does. If it's sickness, bring it to God. If it's trying to make ends meet, bring it to God.

God will help you to manage your stress, but you have to lay it in His hands and trust Him to help you fix it. Whatever it is, it's not too big for God to help you to manage. Whatever it is, it's not too overwhelming for God to help you to cope with. Stress. Worry. Loss of sleep. Give them to God and watch Him bring you out.

CHAPTER SEVEN

When You Can't See Your Way Clear, Part 1

―――⊰⊱―――

READ THE SCRIPTURE: Psalm 69:1-13

Save me, O God,
 for the waters have come up to my neck.
I sink in deep mire,
 where there is no foothold;
I have come into deep waters,
 and the flood sweeps over me.
I am weary with my crying;
 my throat is parched.
My eyes grow dim
 with waiting for my God.

More in number than the hairs of my head
 are those who hate me without cause;
many are those who would destroy me,
 my enemies who accuse me falsely.
What I did not steal
must I now restore?

O God, you know my folly;
 the wrongs I have done are not hidden from you.
 Do not let those who hope in you be put to shame because of me,
O Lord GOD of hosts;

> do not let those who seek you be dishonoured because
> of me,
> O God of Israel.
> > It is for your sake that I have borne reproach, that shame
> > has covered my face.
> > I have become a stranger to my kindred,
> > > an alien to my mother's children.
> > It is zeal for your house that has consumed me;
> > > the insults of those who insult you have fallen on me.
> > When I humbled my soul with fasting,
> > > they insulted me for doing so.
> > When I made sackcloth my clothing,
> > > I became a byword to them.
> > I am the subject of gossip for those who sit in the gate,
> > > and the drunkards make songs about me.
> > But as for me, my prayer is to you, O Lord.
> > > At an acceptable time, O God,
> > > in the abundance of your steadfast love, answer me.
> > With your faithful help, rescue me
> > from sinking in the mire;
> > let me be delivered from my enemies
> > and from the deep waters.

Some years ago I visited a friend who wanted me to come by and pray with him. And I did. I asked him what he wanted me to pray for and he said, "Derrick, I am in despair, just pray."

At the time I didn't quite understand what that meant. But since that time, which was about twelve years ago, I have a better understanding of what that word *despair* means. To be in despair means to be hopeless, to have no hope, to give up all hope or expectation.

One man said he saw hopelessness displayed in full force as he was driving toward Coast Highway. He said, "While at a traffic light, I was reading the bumper stickers on the car in front of me. One of them had a drawing of a small child on his knees, hands clasped together, looking up. Next to the drawing were the words: 'Nothing fails like prayer.' Next to it was another bumper sticker that read: 'The Next Logical Step is Atheism.'"

To believe that there is nothing but this material world we live in—that there's no God and no "us" beyond this life—is true despair. To believe your situation has no solution, or that God has made a promise and reneged, or that there are no steps worth taking to make your life or circumstances better is true despair.

People who feel this way, who can't see their way clear of their troubles, who believe the answer to what ails them is beyond their reach, don't have hope and don't want anyone else to have hope either. Their blatant shout to others is, "I HAVE NO HOPE, SO HOW DARE YOU HAVE ANY!" Feeling this way is reprehensible. But if you are not careful despair can drive you to this point.

Wishing despair on others is just one of the symptoms you could have experienced trying to fight back your own hopelessness. What are other symptoms? Feeling drained, tired, pooped, bushed—just plumb exhausted. Lack of energy, lack of motivation, difficulty concentrating.

If you have any of these symptoms, you may be in a state of despair. You may feel like you are in a hopeless situation because your path is foggy, and it's difficult to find anything to look forward to. What are some of the reasons you could be feeling this way?

NO ONE CARES

You may feel a sense of hopelessness and can't see your way clear because you don't feel that anyone is genuinely concerned about you or pays you any attention. You may feel that you have to fight and struggle through this life by yourself if you are ever going to have anything, be anything, get anywhere.

A man was sitting next to me in one of the two "husband chairs" in a ladies' clothing store. After thirty minutes and five outfits, the fellow's wife came out of the changing room again. He looked at her and said, "That looks good on you. Get that one."

"Honey," she replied, "this is what I was wearing when we came in."

You may feel that no one is giving you the attention you need. This could be why you are in despair. But there are two other reasons why you could be in a state of despair.

SEEKING IN THE WRONG PLACE

Romans 3:23 says all have sinned and fall short of the glory of God. When any of us sins we should be remorseful, which leads us to repentance. But for some of us this is not the case. For some people an initial sin or mistake leads to regret, followed by some destructive coping mechanism that brings more sin and mistakes, which prompts more regret. On and on the downward spiral goes.

Some of the coping mechanisms we turn to include "drugs, alcohol, overeating, gambling, pornography, escapism, or inappropriate relationships. When we rely on these things to cope with guilt and despair and hopelessness, when we rely on these things to find happiness and satisfaction, we find that regret begets regret - and the cycle continues." (Susan Wilkinson, *Getting Past Your Past*, p. 40)

You may feel a sense of hopelessness because you are seeking to find happiness or satisfaction in something or someone else instead of God. Or you are trying to find happiness and satisfaction in material things. Or you are trying to find happiness and satisfaction by joining a gang or fraternity/sorority. Or you are trying to find happiness and satisfaction in drugs and alcohol. Happiness and satisfaction are not found in any of these things. Make your life worse, that's all they will do.

St. Augustine, one of the giants of the Christian faith, prayed, "Our hearts are restless, until they find rest in thee." Maybe you can't find your way clear because you have not found rest in God—your relationship with God is not right. Your commitment to the Lord is lukewarm, halfhearted, cold as a winter night. So despair has set in; your way is unclear.

But there is something else you need to know to help you analyze your condition so that you can fix it and live a successful life now.

CONTINUOUS PROBLEMS

You may feel a sense of despair because you keep running into problems. Nothing seems to go right. A pulpit committee went to

When You Can't See Your Way Clear, Part 1

hear a prospective minister preach. The thing they liked most about his sermon was that it was only ten minutes long.

They immediately called him as their new pastor. His first week in the new church he preached a thirty-minute sermon. The next week his sermon was almost two hours. The deacons met with him and asked him to explain. His response was that the first time the committee heard him preach, he had a new set of dentures in his mouth that hurt him terribly so he could barely preach ten minutes and had to stop talking because of the pain.

The second time he preached he said his dentures felt fine so he preached a normal thirty-minute sermon. They said, "That explains those two sermons, but please explain this last sermon that lasted two hours long."

The preacher said, "That's easy. I got up that particular morning and accidentally put my wife's dentures in my mouth, and when I started talking I couldn't shut up!"

Your despair may be that at every door of your life stands a problem. You have tried to fix it. Then you thought your panacea would be to ignore it, or blame it on someone else, but none of these things have helped. Nothing seems to go right. When one thing goes wrong, everything seems to go wrong.

You have had one problem after another, and there seems to be no end in sight because when you get one problem solved, two come and take its place. You have been beset by problems. You may have tried several things and nothing seems to work. You feel like a chicken with its head cut off, and you're about ready to succumb to your despair. But there is good news. Don't give up yet. Despite your despair, you can live happily ever after. There is an answer.

In Psalm 69:1-3, we hear these words:

Save me, O God,
> for the waters have come up to my neck.
I sink in deep mire,
> where there is no foothold;
I have come into deep waters,
> and the flood sweeps over me.
I am weary with my crying;
> my throat is parched.
My eyes grow dim
> with waiting for my God.

The writer of this Psalm, who we believe to be David, is suffering; he is in despair. Hopelessness, desperation, despondency have set in his bones. (Why? We don't know.) But what we do know is that even God's people will experience seasons of despair, seasons of doubt, seasons of hopelessness. Even God's people can lose sight of the love and grace of God.

David earnestly begs God to relieve him, to save him, to ease his suffering, to make his way clear so that he can find the knob on the door to get out of his room of trouble, his room of despair.

Even though hopelessness has set in his bones, David begins to feel like he can make it, as we see later in Psalm 69, around verse 30. He begins to feel hope and that a brighter day is coming to lift

When You Can't See Your Way Clear, Part 1

him out of his funk, lift him out of despair, out of his anger, out of his annoying situation.

Even though David starts out by wallowing in despair, he eventually begins to see hope. Yes, he starts to see his way clear. Even when things in your life are unclear and you feel hopeless, you can still make it, still succeed, still have brighter days. It is a fact that every day won't be rosy, but you can still live a successful life. The question that knocks at the door now is this: when you can't see your way clear, what do you do so that you can live a successful life?

FOCUS

Don't focus on the problem, focus on God's promises. Focusing on God and not the problem may sound churchy. But this is not sanctimonious hot air. It works. God has everything you need: salvation, love, healing, hope, strength, joy. There is no scarcity in God because He has everything you need. If you want to roll with the punches, cope with adversity, focus not on your problems but on the promises of God.

The Israelites coming out of the wilderness, the parting of the Red Sea, the blind receiving their sight, the five thousand being fed with five loaves of bread and two fish all point to God's promises.

In Psalm 69:22-25, the psalmist says,

> Let their table be a trap for them,
>   a snare for their allies.
> Let their eyes be darkened so that they cannot see,
>   and make their loins tremble continually.

Pour out your indignation upon them,
>and let your burning anger overtake them.
May their camp be a desolation;
>let no one live in their tents.
Furthermore the psalmist says in Psalm 69:29-30,

But I am lowly and in pain;
>let your salvation, O God, protect me.
I will praise the name of God with a song;
>I will magnify him with thanksgiving.

When the psalmist thought of his dismal situation, his numerous enemies, he broke out in fear and wanted to do his enemies harm—or wanted harm done to them. But when he thought about God, he remembered God's promises. He remembered what God said He would do, what He pledged to do, what He guaranteed us He would do. What did God promise you?

God promised that He wouldn't put on you more than you can bear. I know sometimes it may not seem that way, especially when you have multiple problems you are trying to deal with at the same time. But no matter what mayhem you are in, God promised you would be able to stand up under the weight. He promised not to put so much on your shoulders that you buckle under it. Perhaps you are thinking this is vacant verbiage, idle talk. But it's not.

First Corinthians 10:13 and 2 Corinthians 12:9 are your proofs: "No testing has overtaken you that is not common to everyone. God is faithful, and he will not let you be tested beyond your strength, but with the testing he will also provide the way out so that you may be

When You Can't See Your Way Clear, Part 1

able to endure it." And, "'My grace is sufficient for you, for power is made perfect in weakness.' So, I will boast all the more gladly of my weaknesses, so that the power of Christ may dwell in me."

As I reflect on these Scriptures, I recall that during a men's meeting at my church people were asked to volunteer for a project, and Ronnie McCullough, one of my members, raised his hand to volunteer. I looked over at him and said, "You are taking on too much. You are already doing several things, involved in several ministries at Kelley Chapel. Don't overload yourself."

He replied, "I just believe God won't put on me any more than I can bear."

Mr. McCullough understands one of God's promises. God promised not to put on you more than you can bear.

Under your own strength life events are unbearable. Moreover, trying to cope with life without God heightens your frustrating sense of helplessness. But with God the things you do—the laborious and time-consuming events you encounter in this life—are bearable, meaning you can manage and endure them.

God promises not only to give you what you can bear but also to finish in you what He started. Philippians 1:6 says, "He who began a good work in us will complete it." God's work for you started a long time ago when Jesus died on the cross in your place. His work in you continued when you confessed with your mouth and believed in your heart that Jesus is Lord.

The work that God began in you, molding you into what He

Living A Successful Life Today

wants you to be, making you more like Jesus, enabling you to live according to His kingdom principles (which blesses you when you do), He is not going to stop until one day when He calls your number for you to come and meet Him face-to-face.

You can live a successful life, but guilt, doubt, and paranoia will try to rob you of this promise. So every day remember God promised that He is going to complete the work He started in you. We see this in Job's life.

Job was a seasoned leader and wealthy man living in a land called Uz with his large family and extensive flocks. He was "blameless" and "upright," always careful to avoid doing evil (1:1). One day, Satan ("the Adversary") steps in front of God's throne. As Satan stands there, God boasts to Satan about Job's goodness, but Satan says Job is only obedient and good because the Lord continues to bless him. "Take Your hands off him," says Satan, "and I bet he will curse You." God allows Satan to plague Job with problems, but He forbids Satan to take Job's life in the process.

One problem after another comes at Job, but even in his turbid and restless state, Job never curses God. He gets weak at times. On the surface of his life, you can see the wear and tear, but his core is never shaken; his faith in God never dithers. In fact, on one occasion when Job appears to be at his wits' end he cries out, "Though he slay me, I will trust in him." On another occasion he cries out, "When he has tried me, I shall come out like gold."

God promises that your trials will make you stronger. He

promises that if you trust in Him whatever trials come your way, whatever evil comes your way, whatever disappointments come your way, He will use them to build up your faith. That's right, build your faith. I don't know about you but I need that.

I don't need my problems to crush me and permanently wound me and forever scar me. I need my trials to do what Jesus said they would do: build up my faith. I remember when I ran track, and I was trying to get my legs stronger so I could run faster and longer.

My track coach would make me run hills. The more I ran those hills the stronger my legs became; I had more endurance. I could run longer distances. I could perform better. I could run faster.

Trials for the children of God are like running hills; they make us stronger; they give us more endurance; they give us the stamina to endure suffering longer—and overcome it. This is what God promises trials will do for you—not defeat you if you trust Him, not break you down if you trust Him. But give you greater faith.

So to see your way clear to the other side of the trouble standing in front of you or the trouble you are going through, don't focus on the problem but focus on God's promises. God's promises are lampposts along the street of Trouble Road that guide you through to the next street, which is called Deliverance Blvd.

Yes, God makes the way clear when you focus on what He said He would do, when you focus on God's blessings and His goodness and wonder-working power. Center your attention on God's guarantees because that's how you harness His power, clear your way, and live a successful life.

The Bible says in James 1:2-4,

> Consider it pure joy, my brothers and sisters, whenever you face trials of many kinds, because you know that the testing of your faith develops perseverance. Perseverance must finish its work so that you may be mature and complete, not lacking anything.

I like the way it reads in *The Message* translation.

> Consider it a sheer gift, friends, when tests and challenges come at you from all sides. You know that under pressure, your faith-life is forced into the open and shows its true colors. So don't try to get out of anything prematurely. Let it do its work so you become mature and well-developed, not deficient in any way.

GOD'S PRESENCE

But this is not all. There is another coping skill you can use to help you see your way clear. Have you ever seen the movie *It's a Wonderful Life* starring Jimmy Stewart? Many years ago, Jimmy Stewart shared the story about the filming of that movie.

> It's hard to explain, he said, I, for one, had things happen to me during the filming that never happened in any other picture I've made. In one scene, for example, George Bailey is faced with unjust criminal charges and, not knowing where to turn, ends up in a little roadside restaurant.

He is unaware that most of the people in town are arduously praying for him. In this scene, at the lowest point in George Bailey's life, Frank Capra was shooting a long shot of me slumped in despair.

In agony I raise my eyes and, following the script, plead, "God . . . God . . . dear Father in heaven, I'm not a praying man, but if you're up there and you can hear me, show me the way. I'm at the end of my rope, show me the way, God. . . ." As I said those words, I felt the loneliness, the hopelessness of people who had nowhere to turn, and my eyes filled with tears. I broke down sobbing.

This was not planned at all, but the power of that prayer, the realization that our Father in heaven is there to help the hopeless, had reduced me to tears. (*Guideposts*, December 2005, p. 82)

Another coping tool to help you when you struggle to see your way clear is not to forget that God is present to help you. All kinds of sensations—possessed, obsessed, compulsive—will run through you when you forget this. The Lord said He is a "very present help in a time of need." Don't forget that.

Coming out of heaven, taking off His divine nature, putting on frail human flesh, and encountering everything we experience—hate, bitterness, rage, jealousy, betrayal, suffering, pain—God didn't do this to bring destruction to you; He could've done that from heaven. He didn't come into the world to destroy you; He came to help you, to direct your footsteps, to get you over the hump, to help you see that with Him on your side all things are possible. God is present with you.

Since God is present, you should persevere. In this life you will be damaged. You may feel needy; you will make mistakes. But you should persevere despite these times because God is with you. Problems are a part of this life, but you have to keep trying.

Then, to see your way clear, make sure you talk with God daily. Psalm 69:13 says, "But as for me, my prayer is to you, O LORD. At an acceptable time, O God, in the abundance of your steadfast love, answer me with your faithful help."

Talk to God daily, and when you talk with Him do what David does. Give Him your prayers and let Him decide how He needs to respond to your request: the best time to respond, the best place to respond, the best way to respond.

This will give you peace of mind. As long as you are standing in one spot waiting for God to hand you something you asked for—and the exact time you want it—you are going to be on edge, you are going to be stressed out, you are going to be filled with anxiety.

To see your way clear, remember your time and God's time are different. When you think it best for God to do something—rescue, fix a situation, mend a relationship—may not be best.

The Lord says in Isaiah 55:8-9,

> "My thoughts are nothing like your thoughts," says the LORD.
>   "And my ways are far beyond anything you could imagine.
> For just as the heavens are higher than the earth,
>   so my ways are higher than your ways and my thoughts
>   higher than your thoughts."

When You Can't See Your Way Clear, Part 1

Do you hear what that scripture says? It says God does things according to His will and not yours. That doesn't mean He doesn't consider what you say or ask, but it is analyzed alongside His will. If your prayer is in line with His will then it is granted. If it is not then it is not granted. God does whatever He does according to His thoughts. The story about Lazarus illustrates this point.

The Bible tells us about a man named Lazarus. He was sick and his sister Mary sent for Jesus to come heal her brother. But Jesus didn't come right away, at the time Mary thought He should. Jesus took care of some other business He had to attend to. So while Jesus was doing these other things Lazarus died.

When Jesus arrived, Mary said to Him, "If You had been here, come when I called You, he would not have died." Jesus looked at Mary and then looked at the tomb where Lazarus lay and said, "Lazarus, come forth." And Lazarus stood up and came forth.

The Lord responds when He gets ready to respond, and whenever that is, it will always be on time. So when life is unclear and you feel hopeless, remember God is present. And since He is present talk to Him and give Him your prayers by praying,

> Lord, let Your will be done.
> Lord, fix it when You get ready.
> Lord, fix it how You want it fixed.
> Lord, come to my rescue, my deliverance, when You think the time, the situation, and the conditions are right.

Living A Successful Life Today

David said in verses 32-33, "The humble will see their God at work and be glad. Let all who seek God's help be encouraged. For the Lord hears the cries of the needy; he does not despise his imprisoned people."

David said, "Answer me I pray, O, Lord. It's time for a break! And God, answer in love!" David knew that in due time God would come through. He would deliver. He would set him free from what had him bound.

Your situation may be that you have given up, but the word of the Lord for you is that He will come through. You have traveled with God this long. So don't lose your nerve now. Don't feel you are fighting a losing battle now. Your situation is not a lost cause.

I once read about a woman placed in an institution in 1929 because of a nervous breakdown. She had left her native country and come to America with hopes and dreams. Unfortunately, nobody could speak her language. She languished there for forty-eight years. Still, in all that time, nobody was able to understand her.

It appears they had given up on her. It would appear she had lost all hope of her original dream. To those in the institution she was a hopeless case. To them she simply existed in her own little world.

Then one day came breakthrough. In 1972, a multilingual caseworker by the name of John Kurz began to talk with her. Kurz was a caseworker from the Bureau of the Aging. Not only did he understand her language, but he also found out her name Mary Peischl. Kurz also found out that she had left what was the former

Austro-Hungarian Empire when Franz Joseph I was in power. Kurz even helped her to reunite with her five children. Do you see what happened?

The Lord came through this caseworker to set this woman free from her prison of hopelessness. Imagine for just a minute that you were this woman. Imagine that people had written you off as hopeless. Then imagine that one day there was a breakthrough for you just as there was for this woman. (Paraphrased from *Tarbell's Teachers' Guide*. 86th Annual Volume. Edited by Dr. William P. Barker. Elgin: David C. Cook Publishing Co., 1990, p. 248)

Keep believing and in due time you will be delivered. Keep believing that sooner or later things are going to work in your favor. Everything around you may tell you differently, that there is no way your situation can be changed, that the odds are against you, that you are at a point where you don't even have enough rope left to tie a knot and hold on, but you have to keep believing that your daybreak is coming.

You have every reason to believe that troubles don't last always. You have every reason to believe that weeping only tarries for a night. Why? Because you thought your situation couldn't change the last time God delivered you. You thought you couldn't be delivered from your lions' den the last time God protected you. When a crisis came into your life the last time, you thought it was over. But you are still standing, still praising His name.

You have all the proof you need to believe that God is going to come through for you. The devil may be telling you right now that God won't. He won't come through. He won't deliver. But the devil is a liar—and you know it.

He may tell you nobody cares because he wants you to doubt God. But don't believe the devil; he is a liar. You know it. He may tell you there are some things that God can't do. The devil is a liar. He told you the last time you couldn't see your way clear that you were a failure. But you didn't believe him then. So don't believe him this time; don't put any credence in what he says.

Instead believe that in due time, very soon, before you know it, your change is coming to deliver you from the situation that entangles you and has you wondering if God still loves you.

God does still love you, so stop believing that He doesn't. He still cares. He is still concerned about you and wants the best for you every day of your life. You may be unable to see your way clear from whatever is in front of you, from whatever is on your back, from whatever is stealing your joy, but the way to get through it, the way to overcome it, is to keep believing that in due time something good is going to happen to you.

Your change is coming. That is what you have to hold onto. When you feel hopeless, when you feel in despair, continue to believe that things are going to get better. The situation is going to turn around. Your enemy will be conquered. Your emptiness will be filled. Your way will be made straight. Keep believing, no matter what is going on in your life, that God is working things out for you.

CHAPTER EIGHT

When You Can't See Your Way Clear, Part 2

READ THE SCRIPTURE: Psalm 69:1-13

Save me, O God,
    for the waters have come up to my neck.
I sink in deep mire,
    where there is no foothold;
I have come into deep waters,
    and the flood sweeps over me.
I am weary with my crying;
    my throat is parched.
My eyes grow dim
    with waiting for my God.
More in number than the hairs of my head
    are those who hate me without cause;
many are those who would destroy me,
    my enemies who accuse me falsely.
What I did not steal
    must I now restore?
O God, you know my folly;
    the wrongs I have done are not hidden from you.
Do not let those who hope in you be put to shame because of me,
    O Lord GOD of hosts;
do not let those who seek you be dishonoured because of me,
    O God of Israel.
It is for your sake that I have borne reproach,

> that shame has covered my face.
> I have become a stranger to my kindred,
> > an alien to my mother's children.
> It is zeal for your house that has consumed me;
> > the insults of those who insult you have fallen on me.
> When I humbled my soul with fasting,
> > they insulted me for doing so.
> When I made sackcloth my clothing,
> > I became a byword to them.
> I am the subject of gossip for those who sit in the gate,
> > and the drunkards make songs about me.
> But as for me, my prayer is to you, O LORD.
> > At an acceptable time, O God,
> > in the abundance of your steadfast love, answer me.
> With your faithful help, rescue me
> from sinking in the mire;
> let me be delivered from my enemies
> and from the deep waters.

Has there ever been any time in your life that you've felt up to your neck in trouble? You may be feeling that way right now—up to your neck in trouble with sharks swimming around your feet as you tread water and hang on to whatever you can for dear life. Right now you may feel like troubled waters are about to overtake you, about to choke you. What would make a person feel like this?

OBSESSED

In Herman Melville's *Moby Dick*, Ahab is obsessed by the white whale that took his leg. He is compelled to chase the whale, to seek vengeance. As you read the book you say to yourself, "Oh let it go, you can live with one leg, but seeking revenge may cause you a greater price."

But Captain Ahab, foaming at the mouth, can't see this. Why? Because he is obsessed. So he goes to the deep, and to his death, strapped to the back of the white whale, strapped to the back of the obsession he let steal his life.

Obsession can be a fatal flaw. It will cause you to forget yourself, lose your reserve, your temper, or your self-restraint. Some people can't see their way clear because they are obsessed with some idea, some philosophy, or some person that is detrimental to them. And it's not like people don't try to warn them. For you see, they try to tell them to let go. But the warning falls on muted ears or the person flies off the handle.

In the last chapter I highlighted Psalm 69. I'm highlighting it again in this chapter because it still has more incisive instructions to give you about seeing your way clear when things seem difficult. Verse 1 says, "Save me, O God, for the waters have come up to my neck."

As I said in the first part of this teaching, David felt up to his neck in trouble, hoarse from crying for help. Why? We don't know. But whatever it was—family problems, marital problems, strained relationships, drinking problems, depression, unhappiness, confusion—it had David feeling as if a wave were getting ready to take him under.

Nevertheless, as you keep reading this Psalm, it doesn't show us that the flood of trouble engulfed and drowned David; it shows us that David managed to swim clear to dry ground, to a safe area where he could catch his breath, rest, and get his energy back. Even when things in your life are unclear, even when you may feel like trouble is covering you from head to toe, you can still make it, still succeed, still have brighter days, still get to dry ground—a safe place. But you have to know what to do when you can't see your way clear.

In the last chapter, I gave you a few things you can do when you can't see your way clear because God tells us in the Bible that we can prevail; we just have to learn how and when to implement strategies that will help us get through the fog of uncertainty to the victory. Even when troubles are standing front and center in your life, you can overcome. You can be victorious even when your way is not clear. So what do you do?

TAKE THEM TO GOD

When you can't see your way clear, take your problems to God. Don't let your troubles force your hand and cause you to do something stupid. To the Lord is where your troubles or problems or burdens need to go, not to a friend, not to a bottle, not to drugs, not to a sister or brother or children.

Furthermore, you don't need to set them on a shelf thinking they are going to get better as the clock ticks and the days go by because human problems seldom get better on their own when they have been allowed to become infected with anger, resentment, hurt, and revenge. Stop pacing the floor. Stop wondering what you are going

When You Can't See Your Way Clear, Part 2

to do next. When you can't see your way clear, take your problems to God.

Get a load of what David said in Psalm 69 when he was in trouble. He said in verse 1: "Save me, O God, for the waters have come up to my neck." To God your problems should go. Is there anyone better? Your problems should be laid on His table.

You can't fix them by yourself; the problem may be too big; it may be too complicated for you; you might have let it fester too long without getting help, and now the wound is gangrenous. You need a doctor now. In fact, you need a surgeon with a steady hand to cut the problem out without killing you and disrupting your household or your life so that you will be able to go on and live a healthy life, a productive life, a life that is not wounded and wounds others whom it comes in contact with.

Your problems need to go directly to God because you can't fix them. That's right, I said you can't fix them. You think you can. But you need to understand something: fixing your car is not like fixing your life. Fixing your vacuum cleaner is not like fixing your life. Fixing your child's bicycle is not like fixing your life.

Your life is much more complicated. It has gears you have never seen. It has equipment you don't even know you have yet. It has parts that would blow your mind if you knew you had them. You make your life worse when you get in there tampering with it, and because you don't know what you are doing you permanently break something.

And so your relationships become loose-screw relationships. Your life becomes a loose-screw life. That's why I'm telling you that you better get a move on it and put your problems on God's table because you don't know how to fix them, but He does. Give your problems to God; there are all kinds of trouble you will deal with in this world that you can't foresee, but God can.

Some of it is because we live in a fallen world. A world that was perfect, with no sickness, no death or disease, but fell because of Adam's sin, and as a result the world has to contend with sickness, sorrow, evil, and death. Because of the fall, everyone born into this world has the sin nature already in him or her. Therefore, nobody is born innocent and pure, but has the inbuilt desire to sin.

We deal with all kinds of trouble in this world. Some of it is because we live in a fallen world. Some of it people bring to us. But some of the trouble is not brought on us by someone else. Some of it we bring on ourselves. There may be a problem you are dealing with right now that you brought on yourself. And like so many of us, you tried to fix it yourself to no avail.

There is a biblical story about Abraham I love that illustrates so vividly why it is important for us to give our problems to God. The Bible tells us that one day God told Abraham to take his son Isaac up on Mount Moriah and sacrifice him. If God had told any of us to do that, we would have gone ballistic. But Abraham didn't do that. He didn't let God's request send him into a tailspin.

Abraham did as he was told and took his son up on Mount

Moriah. As they made their way to Mount Moriah, Isaac said to his father, "Father, I see the wood for the sacrifice but where is the sacrifice?" And Abraham kept saying to his son "God will provide."

After Abraham arrived at the destination where he would sacrifice his son, he laid Isaac on the altar. After he raised the knife over his son's body, just as he was about to plunge the knife through his son, the angel of the Lord called out to him from heaven, "Abraham! Abraham!"

"Here I am," he replied. "Do not lay a hand on the boy," the angel of the Lord said. "Do not do anything to him. Now I know that you fear God, because you have not withheld from me your son, your only son."

Abraham looked up and there in a thicket he saw a ram caught by its horns. He went over and took the ram and sacrificed it as a burnt offering instead of his son. So Abraham called that place The Lord Will Provide.

Lay your problems on God's table because He knows when, where, why, and how to fix them. You see, if we had been testing Abraham's faith like God was, some of us would have stopped Abraham as he was climbing the mountain to sacrifice his son. Some of us would have stopped him from sacrificing his son when he put Isaac on that sacrificial slab.

And both of these moments would have been wrong, would not have strengthened Abraham's faith, would not have given Abraham the kind of faith he would need to become the man God wanted him to be, would not have given Abraham the faith to finish the journey God was going to take him on.

God knew the right moment to bring Abraham's test to an end, the right moment that would mature Abraham, the right moment that would make Abraham a better solider for the army of the Lord.

God knows the right kind of medicine to use, and how much. I used to hear the preacher say, "He's a doctor who's never lost a patient." As a boy, I didn't know what that meant. But I know now. It means that God knows when and where and why and how to fix whatever problem you may have. That's what puzzles so many about God's grace, love, and mercy. It never comes too late. It is always ahead of our need.

So that is why you need to lay your problems on His table, lay your troubles that have become dirty and infected and gangrenous on His table and let God operate; let Him do the surgical procedure so that you can begin to mend from your open wounds. No problem is beyond His knowledge to fix. No problem is too sick for Him to cure. No problem's gash is too deep for Him to close. When you go to God for help, He will go to great lengths to help you find relief.

ADMIT YOUR FEELINGS

When you can't see your way clear, not only should you take your problems to God but also admit how you feel. In Psalm 69:7-8 David says, "It is for your sake that I have borne reproach, that shame has covered my face. I have become a stranger to my kindred,

When You Can't See Your Way Clear, Part 2

an alien to my mother's children." This is how David felt about his suffering, and he let God know it.

A flight attendant was giving the standard safety briefing to the passengers. She had just finished saying "In the event of a water landing, your seat cushion may be used as a flotation device" when a man remarked, "Hey! If the plane can't fly, why should I believe the seat can float?"

When you can't see your way clear, admit to God how you feel; there is no need to hide it. If you don't feel good about your situation, tell Him that your situation is getting the best of you, causing you to lose your faith, causing you to worry too much because you feel that God has abandoned you or doesn't care or has put too much on you, and as a result you feel like your faith is about to bundle under. If you feel like you are about to fall apart, tell Him. If you feel alone—and I don't care who you are, at times you feel alone—tell God.

You might as well because He already knows. Psalm 139:1-4 says,

> You have searched me, LORD,
>   and you know me.
> You know when I sit and when I rise;
>   you perceive my thoughts from afar.
> You discern my going out and my lying down;
>   you are familiar with all my ways.
> Before a word is on my tongue
>   you, LORD, know it completely.

All of us like our privacy, but we can't be private with God. He can plumb our psyche. He already knows everything about us: the good, the bad, the ugly, the wounds, the idiosyncrasies, the quirks and habits and peculiarities and eccentricities. Matthew said it like this in his Gospel: "And God knows even the hairs on our heads...."

Admit how you feel to God not only because He already knows but also because it is a part of the healing process. A lot of times we never deal with our issues because we don't admit to anyone, not even God, that we have an issue slinging away at us, repeatedly pounding us in vulnerable parts of our lives.

Perhaps we do this, as I said earlier, because we want the door of our lives shut and locked; we want privacy; we don't want people in our business. And that's understandable because a lot of times people want to get in your business to meddle, not to be helpful but to pry, not to be supportive but to interfere.

And so the result is we are always protecting our privacy by not talking when we really need to, not letting anyone get close to us to help us untie the knots in our lives.

When it is difficult to trust people, when you don't have someone you feel comfortable talking to, God is the one you can depend on. You don't get healed by not talking to God. You don't get better, better in your relationships, better in how you handle yourself, and better at dealing with crises in your life, by pushing God away or avoiding Him.

Talking to God is a part of the healing process; it helps you to

When You Can't See Your Way Clear, Part 2

begin to see your way clear; it will help you to work through your anger and frustration; it will help to uncomplicate your life. For Jesus said, "Come to me, all you who are weary and burdened, and I will give you rest. Take my yoke upon you and learn from me, for I am gentle and humble in heart, and you will find rest for your souls. For my yoke is easy and my burden is light."

I like the way this is said in *The Message* translation:

> Are you tired? Worn out? Burned out on religion? Come to me.
> Get away with me and you'll recover your life. I'll show you how to take a real rest.
> Walk with me and work with me—watch how I do it. Learn the unforced rhythms of grace.
> I won't lay anything heavy or ill-fitting on you. Keep company with me and you'll learn to live freely and lightly.

Admitting how you feel helps you heal, clears up the fog, and sees you forward.

ASKING FOR HELP

Once you tell God how you feel ask for help. The Helpline Center mission is "making lives better by giving support, offering hope, and creating connections all day, every day." Prayer is like a helpline. So use it. Ask for help.

In Psalm 69:13-17, the Bible says,

> But as for me, my prayer is to you, O Lord. At an acceptable time, O God,

> in the abundance of your steadfast love, answer me.
> With your faithful help rescue me
> from sinking in the mire;
> let me be delivered from my enemies
> and from the deep waters.
> Do not let the flood sweep over me,
> or the deep swallow me up,
> or the Pit close its mouth over me.

There is nothing wrong, as I said, when you pray, right off the bat, telling God how you feel, but don't stay in that mood. Some prayers are nothing but complaints, nothing but mourning and groaning "Why me, O God...why did this have to happen to me?" Never moving beyond the complaining and mourning will have you spinning your wheels, stuck in the mud of doubt.

Tell God how you feel and then move to the next step. What is the next? Asking for help. Asking for guidance. Asking for a better view of what God wants you to do. He has a plan for you, and He wants to help you carry it out. Life is a battle, but He wants to see you win.

David says in verses 34-36,

> Praise him, O heaven and earth;
> Also ocean and all things that swim in it.
>
> For God is out to help Zion,
> Rebuilding the wrecked towns of Judah.
> Guess who will live there—
> The proud owners of the land?

No, the children of his servants will get it,
The lovers of his name will live in it.

Do you see that? David mourns and complains, telling God exactly how he feels about his condition that is depressing him and almost getting the best of him because he needs help, relief, deliverance, and none seems to come, but David never completely loses hope in God's ability to come through, God's power to give him a fresh start, a new outlook, a new attitude.

And that's what you have to do when you can't see your way clear. You can mourn and complain. You can tell Him how you feel. You can ask Him for help. But the most important thing is that you not lose hope.

Going in and out of the rainy storm clouds, you may feel like losing hope because you are drenched from head to toes, your life soaked with problems, and streams of debris causing you even more problems. But don't lose hope. Look for it to stop raining. Keep faith that God is going to let you dry out so that you don't get weary in well doing.

Don't succumb to hopelessness, because hope in the Lord always benefits you. When you keep faith in God, no matter what, you will eventually see a startling turn of events in your life and those you love.

There is always a blessing when you hope in the Lord. If you put your hope in anything or anyone other than God, you are going to be disappointed one day. Some of it will be intentional. Some of it will be unintentional because all people are flawed in some way.

And so all of us have it within ourselves to disappoint, to make promises we are unable to keep, to say things we can't live up to. But this is never the case with God. He never disappoints. You may feel that He does because you don't always get exactly what you ask for.

But your disappointment will melt away if you realize that God can see your whole future with a blink of His eyes, and He may not have given you what you asked for because it would have thrown you off course, taking you away from His ultimate plan for you, leading you down a road of destruction that would have destroyed you and those around you.

God never disappoints. If you trust in Him, He always in some way rewards your trust, rewards your faith, rewards your confidence in Him. This is what the songwriter was saying to us when he wrote his famous song:

> My hope is built on nothing less
> Than Jesus' blood and righteousness.
> I dare not trust the sweetest frame,
> But wholly trust in Jesus' Name.
>
> On Christ the solid Rock I stand,
> All other ground is sinking sand;
> All other ground is sinking sand.

People can disappoint or forever put us on hold, but God never will. Hope in Him always leads to rewards. Proverbs 3:5-6 says, "Trust in the LORD with all your heart and lean not on your own understanding; in all your ways submit to him, and he will make your paths straight."

Psalm 2:12 says, "Blessed are they who put their trust in him."

Psalm 23:5 says, "God prepares a table before me in the presence of my enemies.

He anoints my head with oil; my cup overflows."

People can let you down. But God always gives us unwavering support. He will never abrogate being there for us. We never have to say to God "put up or shut up." He never makes a promise and reneges. It is not in His DNA: his genetic makeup. Rain or shine, don't lose hope in God because hope in Him leads to rewards, not defeat, not punishment, not dissatisfaction but blessings that lift you when you are down in the dumps, blessings that help you to overcome all that would endeavor to crush you, and blessings that give you the authority and strength and boldness you need to be a conqueror.

Never losing faith in God, that is what helps you to keep going when you can't see your way clear. Have hope in Him. Have confidence in Him and your reward will come, your blessings will come, your answers will come.

That's what the Word of God tells you: have confidence in God even when people try to rain on your parade, and your obstacle will be removed. Have confidence in God, and your hurts will be healed and your soul satisfied. Your way may be dark and rainy right now, but never lose hope. And whatever it is, whatever is bothering you, God will work it out for your good.

Guidelines for Leading a Study of
Living a Successful Life Today, Part 1

In this book, Derrick R. Rhodes shows how God can help you live a successful, prosperous life. To help churches, businesses, community organizations, and individuals facilitate a discussion group, this study guide was developed to help the book be beneficial for all who are looking to be what God planned for them to be. The following are steps that can help:

1. Give the purpose for the meeting, which is to do a group study of this book.
2. Allow all participants to introduce themselves.
3. Hand out the book to all participants before the first meeting so they can read the Introduction: Living a Successful Life. Do not allow the group to be too large because it will hamper full involvement from the total group.
4. In the same meeting where you hand out this book, set a beginning time and ending time for each session, and stick to the time.
5. Begin each session by reading the purpose of each chapter or give your own overview.

6. Read the book first and develop study questions for each chapter. The study questions will be used during your group discussion.
7. In the first meeting also establish the following ground rules:
   a. During the discussion, there are no wrong answers.
   b. The person who has not spoken will be allowed to do so before others who have already spoken are allowed to speak again.
   c. No one should be interrupted unless the leader sees it is time to give someone else an opportunity to speak.
   d. Make it known that all participants are expected to attend all sessions.
   e. There are nine chapters, so the study can last for nine weeks.
8. As the leader, be sure to keep the conversation moving, encourage participation, and thank participants for their answers.